WITTGENSTEIN
LANGUAGE
&
PHILOSOPHY

warren shibles

Wisconsin State University—Whitewater

WITTGENSTEIN LANGUAGE & PHILOSOPHY

WM. C. BROWN BOOK COMPANY
An Affiliate of
WM. C. BROWN COMPANY PUBLISHERS ■ Dubuque, Iowa

13284

By the same author:
Philosophical Pictures

This book is a collection of essays on Wittgenstein but they do not all do the same thing. In the first essay it is seen that one of his main contributions to philosophy is that of his unique style and his way of philosophizing. The second essay shows how his method gives insight in a way similar to that given in poetry. The third essay is directed toward Wittgenstein's notion that when ordinary language goes on a holiday people get misled. It is seen that this is exactly what happens to Alice in *Alice in Wonderland* and it happens as she continually bumps her head against the limits of language. The chapters on memory and intention rely heavily on what Wittgenstein says about these concepts but include alternate and more recent statements as well. The last chapter shows the relation between Zen and ordinary-language philosophy and in doing this further reveals something about Wittgenstein's method of doing philosophy.

Wisconsin State University— Warren A. Shibles
Whitewater

Table of Contents

Although Wittgenstein bases his philosophy on ordinary language his own language is by no means ordinary. It is, however, so revealing, that an attempt will be made here to show that his style rather than other aspects of his later work is one of his greatest contributions to philosophy.

Although von Wright[1] asserts that Wittgenstein had no predecessors, his philosophy may be seen as a working out of Dewey's pragmatism. In addition, W.M. Urban[2] had developed concepts closely resembling those of the *Investigations*. Since Urban's philosophy of language is not widely known, a brief outline follows. For Urban, words are first learned in an adherent stage wherein the word is closely tied to an object. One might think of a child's utterance "ball" upon seeing one. There is a similarity here to what Wittgenstein calls a paradigm case. In the second stage language becomes metaphorical, for example, the use of "to play ball" meaning "cooperate." In the third stage language becomes symbolic. Here words have meaning as part of a universe of discourse and are no longer simply tied to objects. They may be traced back through the other stages to refer to objects, however. These stages may be thought of as descriptive as well as genetic.

Wittgenstein holds that we learn to use words in certain situations for certain purposes. This yields ordinary language. But there is a difference between talking of learning language as a child and talking of the whole development of language. Urban directs his attention primarily to the development of language when he speaks of the three stages outlined above. If Wittgenstein had referred to the origin of language as ordinary language it would not make sense for him to speak of ordinary language. Ordinary a century ago is by no means ordinary today.

Whereas Urban stresses the mobility, flexibility and metaphorical nature of words not only in the genetic sense but in everyday use Wittgenstein attempts to tie language down to the original, childhood learning situation. If we learn $\sqrt{1}$ in mathematics in a certain way it must be used in that way in the future. It is a misuse of language to deviate from ordinary language or from the original learning situation.

Both philosophers agree that words only have meaning as part of a context or situation. Urban says that in the symbolic stage words have a meaning of their

[1] Norman Malcolm, *Ludwig Wittgenstein, A Memoir,* (London: Oxford Univ. Press, 1958).
[2] Wilbur M. Urban, *Language and Reality,* (London: George Allen & Unwin, 1939).

own and apart from any meaning function or direct reference to objects. They rather have a meaning as part of a universe of discourse. Wittgenstein expresses this by saying that words do not simply name but have meaning only as a part of language and they gain meaning by their use in language. In fact, the meaning *is* the use. What Wittgenstein calls a language-game Urban calls a universe of discourse. By a universe of discourse Urban meant psychology, philosophy, sociology, a conversation between two people, or in general a context of some sort. The notion of language-game is narrower because Wittgenstein rejects the universes of discourse of psychology, philosophy, and language which is not ordinary, that is, which is not used literally as it was learned in the original learning situation.

According to Urban justification or proof and the existence of objects have meaning only as determined by a particular universe of discourse. Physics has objects peculiar to it and methods of justification peculiar to it. Such objects and methods exist only as long as that particular universe of discourse is spoken. Furthermore, the objects and methods of one universe of discourse are different than others. Do not try to find out how much God eats for breakfast or how much he weighs. Physics and religion do not mix. Each universe of discourse has its own methods and to this extent cannot be refuted by another universe of discourse. Do not say ghosts do not exist because you do not see them. You are not supposed to see all of them, some are not visible. Or put another way, if you do see this type of ghost it's not a ghost.

Wittgenstein's language-games also have their own methods of justification, truth and falsity, and their own peculiar terms. Words have meaning and use only as part of a language-game. What Wittgenstein called the learning of a language-game may be expressed in Urban's philosophy as the learning of a particular universe of discourse. We acknowledge meanings and methods in that universe of discourse as we do in a language-game. Wittgenstein wrote, "If language is to be a means of communication there must be agreement not only in definitions but also in judgments." (242)[3]

We may not acknowledge all universes of discourse or language-games, however. We may not all acknowledge meaning in religion, astrology or even physics. Furthermore, language-games and universes of discourse are constantly changing as both philosophers recognize. For example, the concept of "gravity" is rejected in certain mathematical systems of physics. Various new geometries and mathematics arose and also ordinary language changed. This change is recognized by Urban especially. For him language is primarily metaphorical. For Wittgenstein whereas a language-game can change we must try to stick with the literal, original language-games we learned.

The language-games and universes of discourse we learn are based upon our needs and wants or, in other words, on value. We see things in certain ways for

---

[3] Numbers in brackets refer to Ludwig Wittgenstein, *Philosophical Investigations,* 3rd ed., (New York: Macmillan, 1958.)

certain purposes. We create language for our needs and purposes. The comparison of Wittgenstein's philosophy with Dewey's is obvious. Both philosophers stress actual practice, contexts, purposes, language as a tool or instrument with which to do things, and the learning situation. Wittgenstein's notion of philosophy as "therapy" is similar to Dewey's "reconstruction" in philosophy. Whereas Dewey had more and more to recognize the central role of language as a research tool Wittgenstein gave a more detailed analysis of it in its function as a form of behavior.

Wittgenstein does differ from other philosophers in his concern with the particular example, the particular phrasing of a sentence. He juxtaposes words so as to point up absurdities or ordinarily unnoticed aspects. Wittgenstein asks if the order "slab" in slab-language is a word or a call. What does it mean to ask that? Is it the same word as "slab" in our language. No. Slab-language has its own form of life. *In* its language-game "slab" is not the elliptical "slab" of our language. If you think "slab" in slab-language is elliptical for "Bring me a slab," how do you *mean that* while you say "slab!"? That is, how can you say "slab" and mean something else? Here it is suggested that the categories of speech such as imperative, command, etc., are different in different language-games. What is an acceptable command in one language or language-game may be an unacceptable elliptical word or statement in another. The categorization and meaning of a word are determined by the language-game and if this context is ignored errors will supposedly arise.

Urban would have put the general issue in a similar way. There are two different universes of discourse here: (1) slab-language and (2) English. You cannot literally reduce one language to another. On the other hand you can say that "slab" of slab-language when used in English is a metaphor. It doesn't ordinarily belong in English (don't confuse it with the English word "slab") and therefore it becomes a metaphor. Wittgenstein underplays the notion of metaphor and instead concentrates on getting language back into what he calls "ordinary" language. In this way creativity and new insight is diminished. This underplay of metaphor however only accords with his explicit statement. In actual practice, as we can see by Wittgenstein's style of presentation and argument, he is a master at gaining insight by the use of analogy, metaphor and striking juxtapositions.

In a sense Wittgenstein is not presenting an ordinary view at all. He says that if you do not keep the multiplicity of language-games in view you will be inclined to ask such questions as: " 'What is a question?'—Is it the statement that I do not know such-and-such, or the statement that I wish the other person would tell me ...? Or is it the description of my mental state of uncertainty?—and is the cry 'Help!' such a description?" (24) We must supposedly go back and find out in what situation we first used the words "What is a question?" When was it appropriate to utter that sentence? But then under what circumstances did Wittgenstein himself learn to utter the sentences he uses? He rejects philosophical language and claims he does not present a theory. Philosophical statements are merely "grammatical jokes." (111) Yet he both uses philosophical language and presents a theory. He says we must look at the use not the meaning. This places Wittgenstein's own statements in an odd position. He must have been prompted to utter the statements he uttered because of a certain circumstance. One can see here the pragmatic view that we only act when there is a need or problem to be solved. Where and how did Wittgenstein learn to utter the statements he utters? They are philosophical statements yet he rejects such statements because they are divorced from their original context. His statement that meaning is actual use and is not analyzable into descriptions and explanations then would require us to say about his own language that it is or means according to its use. In other words what Wittgenstein meant is what he said and this view is by no means ordinary.

It should be noted that Wittgenstein's *Investigations* form a collection of isolated statements and insights. They are on the same general topic of the philosophy of language, however. He wrote that he tried to organize them better but failed. He calls them "philosophical remarks" and "a number of sketches of landscapes. . . only an album." One reason for this is that he did not think a philosophical theory could be presented but only particular instances and examples. The many aspects of language, he thought, cannot be organized into a single theory, a single thread running through all instances. One can see a general theory in Wittgenstein's *Investigations* but to avoid some contradictions one may also look at it as a series of separate insights and observations about language—a collection of philosophical remarks.

Urban recognizes the importance of metaphor as was mentioned and suggests that when a word usually used in one context or universe of discourse, is employed in another it usually becomes a metaphor and should not be mistaken for a literal word or statement. When so regarded it can allow us to see relationships we had not previously thought of. Note Schopenhauer's metaphor "The world is will," Parmenides' "Being is one," or "Man is a machine," "Thought is language," etc. Nearly all philosophical statements and especially Wittgenstein's are metaphorical, analogical and are striking deviations from ordinary language. Wittgenstein's philosophy may be thought to be an analysis of the metaphor, "Language is a game of chess." The most consistent analogy he uses to explain his views is that of chess playing. He says that the question " 'What is a word really?' is analogous to 'What is a piece in chess?' " (108) One might think of the actual playing of a game of chess as the model upon which he based many of his views about language. Chess is something you do, master, and engage in—an activity in the pragmatic sense rather than asking why in the philosophic sense. Language according to Wittgenstein is like that. Wittgenstein in this respect *does* the why rather than ask the why. To the question what does

Wittgenstein mean we may reply, "He means what he says,"—and the meaning of his own words in the *Investigations* is their use.

Wittgenstein speaks of a picture as holding us captive and perhaps it often does. A picture may be thought of as a central metaphor or model by means of which things are interpreted. We may see events around us, for example, through the eyes of an artist, or as a physicist does, or in terms of a basic metaphor such as "The world and everything in it is mechanical and obeys mechanical laws." Wittgenstein would point out that this is only one model, one picture among many. But on the other hand he himself presents us with one picture—the picture that the meaning of a word is its use in a language-game. This does not mean, of course, that it isn't a useful picture or model. It may, however, hold us captive at times.

We have in Wittgenstein the explicit assertion that philosophy is to be rejected, and the implicit method which is definitely philosophical. By speaking of philosophy as a philosophical joke he suggests that when language is used out of its ordinary language-game or universe of discourse it becomes strange, it becomes a joke if taken literally. Thales' statement "The world is water" if taken literally is a joke as is "Man is a machine." If taken as metaphors or models through which to view the world and man they are no more strange or humorous than is the hypothesis that man evolved from the ocean or that the human body may be analyzed physiologically. Our most useful models and metaphors are at first considered to be merely humorous or strange statements. Wittgenstein's way of asking questions and juxtaposing words which at first glance seem unusual is an example of this. As an instance he expresses his aim in philosophy as "to show the fly the way out of the fly-bottle." (309)

Wittgenstein comes close to explicitly presenting Urban's theory of creative metaphor. In general, however, he rejects metaphor as being a confusion of language games. Certainly one should see a metaphor, as such, and not as a literal statement but it is overly restrictive to deny the value of metaphorical and analogical reasoning by solely reducing language to ordinary language, literal language. The following statements show that the creative use of language *is* recognized by Wittgenstein. Language-games are regarded as models, as metaphors through which we may observe. "Our clear and simple language-games are not preparatory studies for a future regularization of language—as it were first approximations, ignoring friction and air-resistance. The language-games are rather set up as *objects of comparison* which are meant to throw light on the facts of our language by way not only of similarities, but also of dissimilarities." (130) For we can avoid ineptness or emptiness in our assertions only by presenting the model as what it is, as an object of comparison—as, so to speak, a measuring-rod; not as a preconceived idea to which reality *must* correspond. (The dogmatism into which we fall so easily in doing philosophy.)" (131)

Wittgenstein's discussion of understanding suggests that when we have one use of such a word we have merely begun to understand it. We begin to understand a particular philosophy. "Now, I understand it. Now, I see it." You see a picture, an aspect. Consider a metaphor, "The world is water." Do you understand this if you think of oceans? Given a metaphor, an understanding of it involves expanding it—using it in various contexts. Understanding a word is juxtaposing it with others with which it ordinarily is used but also with words with which it is not ordinarily used. You begin to understand a particular philosophy. It is a beginning. "I really understand it now. I feel like I have made these ideas my own." It is a beginning.

A situation, a word, has many meanings then and we should not think there is only one. There is an aspect of Wittgenstein's remarks about language which should be mentioned. By language-game it is meant that language is used in a situation or circumstance. What is this situation or circumstance? It seems to be a physical situation in which words are learned. The physical environment must then be assumed. But on the other hand the words we use have meaning as part of a language and do not directly name or represent physical things. Objects are determined by a particular universe of discourse. To maintain that language arises in a physical situation takes the epistemological primacy away from language and gives it to a physical and even behavioristic world. In Urban's terminology it gives the universe of discourse of physical language primacy over other universes of discourse. In Dewey's philosophy nature, science, and the physical world are taken as given yet his pragmatic method of inquiry is so open that the assumption of nature and the physical world seem gratuitous in view of it. Dewey conceives of an event to be the basic unit of experience and Wittgenstein regards the ordinary language-game as basic. But an open method of inquiry as Dewey advocates is not consistent with one's taking any fixed unit as absolutely comprising experience.

We have in Wittgenstein's remarks, two views, one in which epistemological primacy is given to language as system and another in which primacy is given to the physical situation in which language is learned. Both of these views are combined into the one notion of language-game. The notion of language-game, then, is self-contradictory in that language is given primacy and at the same time physical situations are given primacy. As Wittgenstein stresses first language then situation we obtain a fluctuating view of what he accepts as given. Another way of putting it is that "use" in "The meaning is the use" can mean use in a language system or use in a particular physical situation, or both.

Wittgenstein's concept of language-game in its various senses is not new. But his own use of language and striking juxtapositions of language is a novel and significant method of philosophizing. He not only presents helpful analogies but ones which purposefully mislead us as well. These misleading ones can also tell us a great deal such as do the following:

1. I'm acquainted with Smith.
is not analogous to
2. I'm acquainted with my mind.

1. Inner speech
2. Whispering

1. I multiplied in room 23.
2. I multiplied in my head.

1. I calculated on paper.
2. I calculated in my head.

1. What color is this room?
2. What color is thought?

1. A star flashed through the sky.
2. A thought flashed through his head.

1. I observe my actions.
2. I observe my consciousness.

1. The mind seems able to give a word meaning.
2. The carbon atoms in benzine seem to lie at the corners of a hexagon.

1. Memory
2. Looking down a spy glass.

1. The meaning of a word.
2. The illustration of a story (a mental image or picture).

1. Where are your pencils and books?
2. Where are grief and sadness?

1. Where are your notes?
2. Where are your emotions?

1. Bring me a glass,
2. Bring me a concept.

1. John is the name of a person.
2. "I" is the name of a person.

1. "His face is red" is a description of a person.
2. "I believe" is a description of a person.

In addition to the models, pictures, metaphors, and analogies presented already, Wittgenstein makes use of these false analogies to point up certain absurdities. He once said to his students, "A useful method is to see parallels and to see where they fade. A way of doing this is to produce a fiction."

In addition to this method Wittgenstein phrases questions critically and in a special manner analyzes individual words as well as statements. He asks such questions as "Can you remember what remembering was like last Tuesday?" "Is an *activity* moving?" "What is meant by 'It's on the tip of my tongue'?"

His analysis may be put in the form, "What do thinking and other psychological verbs and nouns mean?" "What does meaning mean?" "What does use mean?" His reply is phrased in terms of metaphors and analogies to chess, mathematics and other models. His questions are usually of the form "What are they like?" e.g. "Is thought like digestion?" "What is sadness?" He suggests, "Sadness is walking down a long grey tunnel." The model may be a word or sentence. We may, for example, think of meaning as an image or, better, we may think of meaning in terms of use. Use may be thought of by comparison with the *activity* of playing a game of chess or the operations *performed* in mathematical calculation. Infinity may be thought of in terms of the notion "beyond" or "one more." These are, of course, only a few ways in which we can interpret what meaning is but in some of these interpretations one word is analyzed or seen in terms of another. A word becomes a model upon which to base an analysis.

As was mentioned Dewey and Urban had already presented much of the theoretical structure contained in Wittgenstein's remarks on language. Meaning considered as use in a language-game was already explored by Urban. What Wittgenstein is important for is not so much his theory as his remarks, his way of thinking in terms of models, of juxtaposing terms to explore their meanings. Juxtaposition of words, analogy and metaphor are seen to be useful methods of philosophical reasoning. What Wittgenstein gave us was a way of philosophizing, a style.

Poetry and Philosophy[1]

With the rise of ordinary language philosophy, the close connection between poetry and philosophy is especially evident. Without attempting here to be comprehensive or to assert exactly what poetry is, it is thought that the poet deals with meanings. He often uses words in unconventional ways by use of juxtaposition, metaphor, analogy, parallel structure and irregular treatment of grammar. In such ways meanings are created, and connotations developed which give insight into the particular subject under consideration. Frequently the words used make sense only if some of their more remote connotations are employed. This is especially true of the more lyrical poets. There is in such poetry, if successful, a singing meaning which comes booming along. I am not reducing lyrical poetry to emotion or feeling. If a poem is in words, as it must be, it *says* something. Its effectiveness and the insight gained is often due to the fact that a unique way is discovered in which to say things and so new things can be said. Poems do not leave you with just feeling without thought. This may be expressed by saying that feeling is one kind of thought. The felt thought, the bloody thought is the one which convinces us, which we take as the true one or supportable one. Nietzsche phrased it, "All truths are bloody truths."

Perhaps a word should be said about the distinction between emotion and reason. Ordinary language philosophers have shown that the distinction is an artificial one if looked at from the point of view of what emotion and emotion words mean and what reason and reason words mean. It has been shown that emotion words such as "envy" in "I envy his technique," have little to do with internal physical or "emotional" states but have to do rather with the context or situation, the relations involved being of a rational sort. The novelist decides whether a person is "angry," "in rage," or "furious" not on the basis of a fictional character's internal states but rather in terms of plot, social relationships, situations and contexts. In other words, it is held that the meaning of emotion words has more to do with their use in language and relational contexts than with internal states. The same analysis applies to reason and reason words. Both emotion and reason words function in language in such a way that, except by artificial convention, there is no absolute distinction between them. They blend in with each other as much as do the two interchangeable sentences, "I 'feel' that this is correct," and "I 'think' that this is correct."

---

[1] This paper was read on October 13, 1967, at the 25th Annual Meeting of The American Society for Aesthetics at Princeton University.

One may also consider a number of individual words and sentences and ask "Is this emotional or rational?" Are, for example, the words "tree," "like," "good," "true," emotional or rational? Consideration of their function or use in language reduces them all to a similar status. What are called emotional words and reason words are to this extent equally comprehensible.

Consider emotion words in such a sentence as "I am *anxious* about their coming." Note that you may have said equally "Let them stay where they are," or "They shouldn't come." Only the first sentence seems to refer to an internal state, "anxiety," but it refers primarily to an external situation as do the second and third sentences.

Do emotion words always refer to a state one has? If so, then what state would "anxious" in "I am *not* anxious about their coming," refer to? A non-existent internal state? For nearly every emotional word or sentence, an equivalent non-emotion sentence could be substituted.

Poetry is an exploration in and with words. In philosophy this might be called analysis. Just as poetry deals with meanings and lays great stress upon language and style, so also does contemporary language philosophy. In this philosophy questions are asked such as "What does such and such a word mean?" What, for example, does "God" or "mind" mean? That is, what would they be like? If you have a mind what is it like? Is it like a solid physical brain containing thoughts somehow, a physical thing "containing" immaterial ones? That leads to difficulties. Is it like a ghost or spiritual entity of some sort? The connection between this search and the poetic one is easy to see. The poet too asks about his subject, "What is it like?" He often, for this reason, uses analogy and metaphor. The philosopher and poet both analyze, for example, man as a machine or man as a spiritual entity. Some philosophies are merely expanded metaphors in a way similar to poems having a basic metaphor. Parmenides' philosophy can be easily analyzed, as Parmendies himself does, in terms of a sphere. Peirce's philosophy can be seen as based on the models of his changing conceptions of logic. Every philosophy can be analyzed into a few basic models or metaphors which are expanded.

It was mentioned that the poet creates meanings; he surprises us with his unusual juxtapositions. The philosopher is now more conscious than ever of the importance of doing the same. Philosophy deals with difficult questions and in order to put in their most significant form they are phrased critically. Critical phrasing, critical comparison—both are essential. Teleology may be crucially put as, "Why is a peach soft?" or "Why does a tree grow up?," "What are your teeth for?," followed by the question, "What are you for?" Consider then how the poet, Dylan Thomas, expressed the teleological issue—"The oak is felled in the acorn/and the hawk in the egg kills the wren." The relationship between nature and man is put by Thomas, "The force that through the green fuse drives the flower/Drives my green age; that blasts the roots of trees/Is my destroyer." The "fuse" and "blast" are connected here and it is and is not a joke. The philosopher, Wittgenstein, might call this "quickening the sense of the queer."

The method of this sort of crucial phrasing and juxtaposition is not peculiar only to ordinary language philosophy. The phenomenologist, Husserl, spoke of the search for his "essences" by means of juxtaposition and concomittant variation. And Royce suggested to James that he try substituting "expedient" for "truth" to yield the strange courtroom oath, "Do you swear to tell the expedient, the whole expedient and nothing but the expedient, so help you further experience." It is, however, true that ordinary language is more alert to this method than are other schools of philosophy. These philosophers as well as poets see the value of exploring the potential and resources or ordinary language.

Wittgenstein presents such questions for discussion as the following:

Is Wednesday fat and Tuesday lean?

What is the correct translation of your wordless thought into words?

Could it ever be 5:00 on the Sun?

The stove is in pain.

Is exact like drawing a chalk line around an area? But the line has breadth.

How is telling done?

I distinctly *remember* that before I was born I. . .

Is a sum in the head less real than a sum on paper?

In what sense have you "got" what you see?

What does a man think for? Because it pays? and compare this with, Does he bring up his children because it pays?

Is hope a feeling? Then is "hope" in "I do *not* hope," a feeling, too?

It is my intention to whistle this theme: have I then already, in some sense whistled it in thought? Wittgenstein explores here the various concepts by putting them in odd contexts. One may compare this method with Joyce's and Gertrude Stein's exploration with language in their works.

A key concept in ordinary language philosophy is Wittgenstein's concept "family resemblances." He says that the meaning of a word is determined by its use and that as it is used in different contexts it has different meanings. These meanings form what he calls "family resemblances." There is no meaning that is the same for every context. But the use one word has in different contexts is what is meant by metaphor. What Wittgenstein sees as "family resemblance" is what the poet sees as metaphor.

Both poet and philosopher engage in the process of seeing an object or situation as now this now that. This process which Wittgenstein calls "seeing as," enables one to explore the diversity of an object to see it in other and perhaps more important ways than those in which it was previously seen. The philosopher, F. Waismann, has suggested that Einstein's theory of relativity was largely based on seeing the concept of "simultaneity" in such a different way. In poetry quite often the "seeing as" process not only involves metaphor or simile but takes the form of an allegory or satire as well.

There is another relationship between poetry and ordinary language philosophy. This comes as a result of the disillusionment with Aristotelian as well as modern symbolic logic. It is now more easy for philosophers to see a poem as an argument on the same level with what goes for a philosophical argument. This trend is in certain respects a return to the pre-Socratic and other philosophies which were written as poems.

Plato said that philosophy cannot be accurately represented in language. Yet he presented his own philosophy in words and sentences. He was, however, careful to tell us that he was giving us a "likely story," telling us only "something like the real case." And he put his philosophy in a dramatic and fictional, not a factual form. Plato in his search for a permanent, absolute, and unchanging reality asserted that language can only yield falsity, it being several stages removed from true knowledge. Yet in order to say that, Plato presented us with myths and metaphors, that is, with a kind of poetry.

Aristotle continued the search for a static, permanent reality and to aid this search established a fixed form, a procrustean logic into which sentences are to be poured—viz. the syllogism. The major difficulties that have been found with the syllogism are, briefly: it assumes what it is supposed to prove (i.e. it is circular), it doesn't yield new knowledge, it makes great use of universal propositions yet very few are to be found, it only concerns quantity and consistency and in so doing distorts ordinary language, fewer assumptions are needed to decide on the conclusion alone than to set up premises which eventually lead to it, meaning is held static for each word (connotations are restricted) in the syllogism which disregards the normal non-static but rather metaphorical use of words. Many of these and similar criticisms apply to symbolic logic also. They are criticisms of logic as well as of its application. One must translate ordinary language into logic and when the symbolic conclusion is reached one must translate back again into ordinary language. In translations both ways the distortion of ordinary language is great and nearly precludes logic as an aid to human reasoning. A similar translation difficulty is to be found in trying to explain mathematical equations in ordinary language. Symbolic logic is very much like mathematics in this regard.

These were some of the difficulties found with logic. On the other hand, logic provides us with an interesting model, however problematic, by means of which we may be able to interpret various phenomena. Logic is an attempt at "seeing as."

As long as logic was of the utmost prominence in philosophy poetry took last place. Poetry was regarded as emotive and of no rational consequent. But with the emergence of the recognition that logic provides us with only one among other models of reasoning, poetry once again is able to come closer to philosophy and even to be of great value to it.

An argument need not and many now think cannot be effectively translated into the "language" of symbolic logic. An argument now is one which is a unified series of statements which give us insight enough to convince us. It is a "bloody" affair not a mechanical one. In this, the poem, and the novel also, provide us with a development and enrichment of meanings leading up to an organized unity of thought and, if successful, a greater knowledge about an issue than we previously possessed. A poem is "convincing" just as much as is a so-called "philosophical argument." An acceptable philosophical argument in ordinary language philosophy may consist of a sentence, e.g. "Consciousness?—but try to see if you can ever catch yourself thinking." This suggestive argument was presented by Wittgenstein to some of his students.

As modern philosophy becomes more conscious of the way thought involves language, it comes closer to poetry which deals intensely with the various subtleties of language and attempts to view in depth similar sorts of inquiries. Poetry and philosophy are both attempts to "learn" our language.

Chapter I
Down the Rabbit-Hole

"And what is the use of a book," thought Alice, "without pictures or conversations." A child's attitude toward words is introduced—What are they really? And why bother with them? (Lewis Carroll (Charles Dodgson) was careful to have his book illustrated.) What begins here is Alice's confrontation with language throughout her adventures.

Alice falls off to sleep and dreams. A dream is itself an odd sort of thing—and perhaps not a thing at that. What it is we never can witness. At the time we dream, we are asleep and not conscious and so cannot be sure we are dreaming. We do not say, "I am asleep and dreaming that. . . ." When we wake and regain consciousness, it is too late to witness the dream for it is gone. Perhaps then we never dream! Perhaps when we wake we are just reporting an experience we then have and erroneously say of it that it is a dream. We do know that when we wake, we tell stories sometimes and begin these with "I dreamt that. . . " or say "I had a dream last night." We are not certain that there are dreams, what "they" are, or when we had "them." Furthermore, if there are dreams, which is real—the dream or our waking state? It is not clear how we can know the answer to this. (It may be noted that a record kept of our rapid eye movements (said to accompany dreaming) cannot show that we dream. The only test is that we report the dreams. And then that it is a dream is still in question.)

The Rabbit takes a watch out of its waistcoat-pocket. But in a dream such things are allowed to happen. And such events if they are or could be dream events differ from real events and so should be put in quotes e.g. "the Rabbit actually took a watch out of its waistcoat-pocket." The quotes indicate that these words are used differently than they are used in our conscious state. If Alice were asked if she saw Lewis Carroll, it would be odd if she answered, "Yes" and when asked "Where?" replied "In a dream." A dream, we usually think, is different than a waking state or illusion that can be corrected. We can't check to see if our dreams are correct. They are supposedly in a different sort of time and space and Carroll exploits that fact. As we saw, we have no direct access, especially while sleeping, to dreams. All we have access to is our report of an experience of some odd sort when we wake up. And it is not clear what the role of memory is or what is being remembered when we supposedly remember having a dream. Remembering a dream is not necessarily like remembering real things. And a dream isn't necessarily a state or something that might be continuous or like conscious experience. Now, Carroll has us in a funny situation by letting his setting for Alice's adventures be a dream.

A dream Alice, who acts like an actual Alice, is chasing a dream Rabbit at no particular time, since dreams transcend our everyday notions of time. (We later find that it is May fourth, but this date occurs in the dream also, and so is not reliable.)

But then if time in a dream is different than normal time there is perhaps nothing wrong with the Rabbit being late. Alice follows the Rabbit in a hole never considering how "in the world," as Carroll puts it, she was to get out. And of course we have a number of worlds: dream, report of dream, real, Alice's and the Rabbit's.

Alice falls into a hole but it is into a dream one in which, like any dream, latitude and longitude and the center of the earth have no longer a usual application. And why not even fall, as she thinks she might, through the earth to the other side where people, she thinks, walk with their heads downwards.

And with a fall like hers through uncertain dream, it certainly would come about that other things would stand upside down too. "Do cats eat bats?" and "Do bats eat cats?" become interchangeable because, as Carroll points out, she can't answer either question. The questions are puzzles which raise significant issues. Are all unanswerable questions alike? Or similarly are all false statements alike? Does a false statement imply a false statement? In symbolic logic, it is a basic principle that a false statement implies ($\supset$) any statement whatsoever regardless of whether it is true or false. Specification and a context is needed, of course, to attempt an answer to the question which Carroll raises.

Alice lands and overhears the scurrying Rabbit say, "Oh my ears and whiskers, how late it's getting!" And here one may suppose this is how a Rabbit would say something similar to our "Oh, my goodness, how late it's getting!" In neither case does the idiom illuminate the causal force. Cause is dream causality here but the first statement still points out how odd causal notions in our everyday descriptions of behavior are.

Alice finding herself in a room of locked doors tries a key and Carroll writes, "Either the locks were too large, or the key was too small." This statement puzzles us. It suggests that the same situation may be described equally in several different ways rather than the single one. We begin to expand further our conventional interpretations and this creates humor but also insight as we will later see. We describe the same event in different ways and create situations by this sort of move. In dreams we can merely dream something into existence. Alice very much wanted to enter a tiny garden but she was too big. She then found a bottle on a table "which certainly was not here before" which allowed her the means by which to change her size. She perhaps dreamt it there. But, too, dream events follow different patterns than normal events and it might have appeared there in some other way. The everyday rules for the behavior of objects and drinking from bottles, Alice learned, may be satisfactory for everyday affairs but not here—not in this "place."

The rules of the dream world are certainly different. After drinking from the bottle she shrinks to a height of ten inches and wonders if she will snuff out altogether like the flame of a candle: "I wonder what I should look like then?" And, of course, since the usual rules and laws of nature as we know them are changed here why not go where the flame goes when the flame goes out. New rules apply but what rules? And perhaps even there are no rules that apply? Or is it that we make the rules to apply and so they must apply? Here, "I wonder what I should look like then?" is a meaningless, disengaged utterance. It misleads us into thinking there is some rule which yields a meaning.

What is the rule for defining one's essence or nature? Alice finds she is now too small to reach the key on the table, and scolds herself, as if she were two people, one scolding, the other being scolded; one giving good advice, the other seldom following it; one scolding, the other crying; one boxing the ears of the other who cheated; playing a game of croquet against herself. We do normally talk as if we are two people but what do we mean? Are we misled by taking some of our expressions too literally? "Well," Alice says, "there's hardly enough of me left to make *one* respectable person!" And the question is thus raised. How can a person be defined? Can he be so numbered as *one* person? Is one just one person only when one is very small? And we may note that in the preceding sentence "one" is used in two places as a synonym of person.

When Alice eats the cake which will either help her reach the key or make her small enough to crawl under the garden door she wants to know which way she is going, smaller or larger. She seems to assume she has two separate selves when she uses the rule of putting her hand on her head to measure her height. With two selves it might work. As it is, she finds she remains the same size. Normally if she grew larger or smaller, this test for height, assuming that a person is only one person, would not work. If one became large so would one's hand and head. An external measure (or other self) would be needed. Even though so many "out-of-the-way things" happen even in dreams, some things might be logically and not merely epistemologically impossible, for example, measuring one's change of height by putting one's hand on one's head.

Chapter II
Pool of Tears

"Curiouser and curiouser!" cries Alice. Grammatical rules change in Alice's state of being surprised. But why not say "Curiouser?" Shouldn't we know what people do not say as well as what they do say? The Rabbit, when Alice asks him for help, "scurried away into the darkness as hard as he could go." Do we say we scurry "hard?" Why not? We do say we run "hard." Why? Does it hurt to run hard but not hurt to run soft(ly)? The reader becomes aware of alternative ways of describing behavior which become "curiouser and curiouser." Certainly language is disengaged from its normal context when Alice speaks of herself as two selves, now in the sense that she has grown so tall that she contemplates sending Christmas presents to her feet.

Alice, starting to introspect says "Let me think: *was* I the same when I got up this morning? I almost think I can remember feeling a little different?" The puzzles here might be (a) do we know we are dreaming when we are dreaming? (b) is telling a dream telling of a feeling or private state one has? (c) how does one know it is a state? (d) one can remember a book or an umbrella but isn't "remember" used in a new strange context in "I remember in a dream" and also in "I remember a dream" (e) do we remember feelings or just ideas?

But the main puzzle, as Alice puts it, is, "But if I'm not the same, the next question is 'Who in the world am I?' Ah, *that's* the great puzzle!" The essence of a person once again is in question. What does constitute a person's being the same? And especially in the dream state, waking state and in light of the idea that the same thing may be variously described according to various conflicting rules and descriptions. What applies in our waking state need not apply in dreams. Who are we in a dream? Ourselves? Someone else? Alice wonders whether she could have changed into any one of her friends.

But there is still another problem—the problem of identity. Alice says, "I can't be Mabel... Besides *she's* she, and *I'm* I." We think that to say a thing is identical with itself is to say something, but it says nothing at all. And to say that two things are identical is nonsense. That is, to say that Alice is identical with Alice does not surprise us. We do not say, "Alice fits nicely into Alice." Nor can Alice be the same as someone else—even an identical twin.

Alice, to see if she is Alice, tries to see if she knows all the things she used to know. But how can one do that? Is the test just to recite what one has been taught in school—and is that knowledge? Is to memorize, to know? Memory may be like dreams in the sense that one cannot now directly witness what happened in the past. Memory must be relied on and memory may be mistaken. We may think we knew something we in fact did not know or vice versa. The question as to whether Alice can accurately remember what she knew is thus raised. It is odd also for Alice, thinking like Alice, to try to remember who she thinks like.

If she doesn't remember what she used to know perhaps she is someone else, e.g. Mabel, she thinks. It is strange that we should think that, that our ideas should be ours and that no one else can have them. Alice thinks that the one whose ideas she has proves that she must be that person. Of course, certain ideas and abilities do characterize certain people. If someone calls down to Alice to come up out of the hole she decides to first ask, "Who am I?" If she likes the person they name she will come up, if not, she will stay down until she is somebody else. The problem of self identity, as well as of knowing, is thus raised.

Alice determines that the fan causes her to shrink again so she drops it. Causality is a difficult concept anywhere. What causal rules apply in Alice's world? Animals are able to talk there but what rules apply to their conversing? Alice tries addressing a Mouse with "O Mouse" because she remembered having seen declined in her brother's Latin Grammar, "A mouse—of a mouse—to a mouse—a mouse—O mouse!" The Mouse just looked back at her inquisitively. In a dream, time is distorted and Alice, in spite of her good knowledge of history, thought the Mouse may have come over with William the Conqueror and that it therefore must speak French. Alice talks to the Mouse as if it were a person. She talks of her soft, nice cat, Dinah, and how it chases mice. Alice has forgotten that the normal rules of conversation don't apply but still isn't sure what rules would apply either. Should one talk of one's pets or rather of astro-physics here? Alice called the Mouse back noticing that its face was pale with passion. And of course that is strange although not because cats eat mice. What would a pale mouse's face look like and what would passion be for a mouse? But further, what does it describe to say a person was pale with passion? But we do say that.

Chapter III

A Caucus-Race and a Long Tail

The question is brought up as to what "it" means when the Mouse said the Archbishop "found it advisable to" go. It's pointed out by the Duck that the word "it" usually stands for or names something. We see however that it does not have that function here. Words do not always just name. They have other uses and functions. The Archbishop did not, for example, find a frog or worm or something else which, the Duck says, would qualify as an "it." Rather he merely found "it" advisable to go.

The Mouse makes the mistake of trying to get the wet ones present dry by telling dry history. Now Alice is the one who begins getting things twisted and twisting them. She looks at the Mouse's tail instead of listening to his tale, mistakes "knot" for "not," suggests that if one loses one's temper her cat Dinah could help find it, mentions in front of a canary, magpie, etc., her cat's prowess regarding birds, tells of how her cat is the best cat in the world (yet there might be something strange about being the best cat in the world which devours poor mice and birds.)

The Dodo raises the question about the purpose and rules of a race. The rules for running it may be set but what is the real purpose of it? In this case it seemed to be to get dry since when all were dry the race was done and the Dodo announced *"Everyone* has won, and *all* must have prizes." But what does it mean to receive a prize when all receive them? It certainly means nothing to win if one cannot possibly lose. "Win" has no use here. To say that all win is to say it is not a race.

The chapter ends with a tale written in the form or shape of an actual tail. Charles Peirce was interested in such forms which convey visual impressions of what is said. Ludwig Wittgenstein's *Tractatus* develops the idea that the structure of language is the structure of the world. Words picture the structure of reality.

Some of the characters appearing in this chapter may be based on the following:

Dodo—Charles Dodgson, because he stuttered and would sometimes begin pronouncing his last name "Do-Do."

Duck—Reverend Duckworth, a friend.

Lory—Lorina Liddell, Alice's sister.

Eaglet—Edith Liddell, Alice's other sister.

Chapter IV
The Rabbit Sends in a Little Bill

The Rabbit looking for his gloves and fan asks, "Where *can* I have dropped them?" And, of course, why not use the possibly more British "can" instead of the more American "could?" "Can" seems stronger than "could," less hypothetical. To note the above use of "can" is to begin to examine the natural laws of the place—if there are natural laws and if it is a place.

As in real life such things happen now as that Alice is given a snapped command "Mary Ann, run home and fetch me a pair of gloves and fan!" and although she is not Mary Ann, she does it. Of course, in this case the command was from a Rabbit. She finds a bottle in the Rabbit's house and concludes that since the bottle she drank from earlier labeled "Drink me" and the cake she ate earlier labeled "Eat me" were interesting, then this bottle, although unlabeled, would be interesting too. Now it would seem that almost anything might happen. It did. She drank and ended up a giant with one foot up the chimney and one arm out of the window.

At this moment Alice again introspects on her condition. Should she have come here? She even in her present plight is filled with wonder and curiosity—curiosity about this new "world," "language," "people." Alice is a philosopher here as she observes with wonder and curiosity. Questions are raised such as What do words really mean? Do we utter disguised nonsense thinking we are saying something deep? Need time be as we usually think it is? Need our natural laws apply? What is causality? In general, need the world be analyzed and thought of by means of the usual patterns and categories? Alice is led into, or dreams into, bumping her head against each of these issues. (Also the psychedelic experience is combined with the dream experience when potions and chemistry of an unusual sort play a role in the story.) The notion of immortality even enters Alice's head when she wonders if she will ever grow old in such a world as she finds herself in down in the rabbit hole. Does one grow old in a dream?

The Alice story began with pointing out that books especially without pictures and conversations aren't very helpful—not for example books with all those fixed truths to learn, jargon and procrustean categories to memorize. They don't help anywhere, especially here. One here must look and see how things happen with a fresh eye. Thus she often talks of learning her lessons, as if they would make her intelligent or would help her out of her dilemma. But one may seriously question if they would help. "Oh, you foolish Alice!" she chides, "How can you learn lessons in here? Why, there's hardly room for *you*, and no room at all for any lesson-books!" In Camus' *Myth of Sisyphus* there is little room for lessons and theory. One must decide for oneself as an individual and absurdity comes anyway. For Camus also one foot is up the chimney and as Alice says, "there's hardly room for you and no room at all for any lesson-books!"

The existential appears here in this form, a form similar to that Nietzsche presented when he attacked education and dry lecturing at students. For Nietzsche every truth must be a meaningful truth, a "bloody truth." (No, there is indeed no room for lesson books here.) The Mouse did give us a model of, as it says, "dry" lecturing. The question "Who am I" which Alice asked earlier certainly also raised the existential question. One should not substitute lessons, rules and memory for reason.

Who is one and how does one act when rules for determining this are absent? The note on the bottle read "DRINK ME" and the rule was clear. Then Alice picked up an unlabeled bottle, a bottle without directions, and chose to drink it. She made the choice. She was beginning to learn her way about in the land of strange rules. She drank no matter what would happen so long as it was interesting, was "bloody" in Nietzsche's sense. And we may compare the label on the bottle with the fact that the "m" on Mouse is capitalized. The names of other animals are also capitalized. "Mouse" indicated both the sort of animal he is as well as his name. His existential being is brought out. We usually don't give mice names. They have no individuality for us in that sense. Furthermore by capitalizing names in this way the question is raised as to the relationship between the thing and the name or label of the thing, the person and the name of the person.

The Rabbit once mistook Alice for his maid Mary Ann, but it is not clear why. Does the Rabbit have poor eyesight or do unusual rules of nature apply? Alice, stuck in the Rabbit's house, was the target of pebbles which turned into cake. She eats one and becomes small again. Her clinging to old rules seems strange when she as a giant threatens to send her cat Dinah to attack the Rabbit. It must have seemed equally strange to the animals since they probably did not know what or who Dinah (the name alone doesn't identify anything) is. When she becomes small again she escapes into a forest and plans her future action. But what can "plan" mean in such a wonderland? What would be the future consequences of any act here? Alice decides according to the rules which used to apply for her that the best thing is "to grow to my right size again; and the second thing is to find my way into that lovely garden." But as Carroll then writes, "She had not the smallest idea how to set about it." She is hungry but is not clear what she might eat. What would nourish her? Certainly not the contents of bottles labeled "Drink Me" or cake. Can we know a priori, as Hume once asked, what will nourish us or do we rather have to wait and see on the basis of experience? In her search for food, Alice finds a mushroom and, as one might not expect, a large blue caterpillar sitting on the top smoking a long hookah.

Chapter V
Advice from a Caterpillar

The Caterpillar asks Alice, "Who are *you*?" and Alice replies, "I know who I *was* when I got up this morning, but I think I must have been changed several times since then." The Caterpillar demands that she "explain" herself. Socrates although not in the story lurks behind the mushroom. What does one mean by "I" or "myself" and how can one, in accordance with Socrates' maxim, "know oneself?" What would that be like? But further Alice says she can't explain herself because she is not herself. The issue is thus again raised of one's knowledge of oneself but it is continued on to the problem of other minds in the following way. When Alice says to the Caterpillar, "Well, perhaps *your* feelings may be different, all I know is, it would feel very queer to *me*." How do we know that the Caterpillar even has feelings or for that matter thinks? But the question has wider reference now because Alice not knowing who she is cannot be sure to which "me" those feelings of direct access belong. She has problems with the existence and nature of mind and feeling other than her own but her own as well.

In asking for an "explanation" for oneself we see that it is an odd thing to ask, Alice asks the Caterpillar who it is and it replies, "Why?" And, as Alice realizes, there is no reason why. The Caterpillar smoking his hookah reminds one of the orient and oriental religious views which see reality as one, there being no certain oppositions, contradictions, or distinctions which are not false. Suppose the

Caterpillar had replied, "I am a Caterpillar." That would be no good. It is socially acceptable but philosophically inadequate. One is not identical with one's name or a role in life.

The Caterpillar insists that Alice recited the poem "Father William" not just not quite right but wrong from beginning to end. It is not certain what it would mean to be *entirely* wrong. If it were entirely wrong, it would not be the same poem. Certainly at least the words "Father William" must be correct.[1] But not to the Caterpillar who appears to think in a different way than does Alice and of course it should—it's not human but a Caterpillar. What Alice regards as a wretched three-inch height, the Caterpillar finds most satisfactory. What to Alice seems obvious is contradicted and seen differently by the Caterpillar. The question is how *do* Caterpillars think? Yes, but also the question how anyone other than oneself thinks may be raised. Is what I call blue the same as what you call blue? How can one ever find that out? How does the Caterpillar know Alice is thinking "one side of *what*?" to reply aloud, "of the mushroom?" To Alice and us, a perfectly round mushroom as this has no right and left side. A perfect sphere similarly has no right and left side. But now the point is also that perhaps to a Caterpillar (who can tell?) the mushroom does have two sides.

Alice eats some of the mushroom causing her neck to become very long. We return to the problem of what one's essence is when the Pigeon takes Alice to be a serpent. Little girls don't have necks that long and Alice, *like a serpent,* does eat eggs. Perhaps we should not refer to Alice as Alice anymore. But what then? What is necessary for Alice to have for her still to remain Alice? It won't do to say that she must have that without which she would not be Alice, because it is just *that,* her essence, which is in question. Poor Alice, no not quite Alice, perhaps not at all Alice. Poor serpent. But serpents are vicious or unfeeling, not poor. Are they? And Alice could not convince the Pigeon of her real nature. Well, who could convince a Pigeon of anything?

Chapter VI
Pig and Pepper

Alice's question "How am I to get in (the door)?" assumes that she is to get in at all. This reminds us of such questions we ask as "Who created the world?" which assumes that somebody did create it. But possibly no one created the world and we don't know what it would be like for a person to create it.

Again Alice makes a mistake by asking of the Cheshire-Cat, "Would you tell me, please, which way I ought to go from here?" The Cat quite appropriately

---

[1] And they are correct. The poem is Carroll's version of Robert Southey's "The Old Man's Comforts and How He Gained Them."

responds, "That depends a good deal on where you want to get to." "I don't much care where—" said Alice. "Then it doesn't matter which way you go," said the Cat, "—so long as I get *somewhere*," Alice added. "Oh, you're sure to do that," the Cat replied, "if you only walk long enough." And, of course, walking "long enough" has nothing to do with getting "somewhere."

As the Cheshire-Cat says everyone there is mad, we have the same situation as with the Caucus-Race. That is, it makes no sense to say anyone is mad where everyone is mad. How would we ever know that *everyone* is mad? The Cat also says that it is mad; and if it is mad we shouldn't take its word for it and if it isn't mad we shouldn't take its word for it. And Alice doesn't at first. The Cat then reasons that if we assume that a dog is not mad (and so there can be no dogs where the cat is), as Alice does, that since it growls when it's angry, and wags its tail when it's pleased and since it (the Cat) growls when it's pleased and wags its tail when it's angry, it (the Cat) must be mad. The definition of madness is not unlike one we usually employ, namely, to be mad is to be unlike other people. This argument is more convincing in showing that the Cat might be mad not because, as Alice points out, a cat purrs and doesn't growl (and it might growl in Wonderland) but because it assumes that a cat is a dog or should be like a dog. There is the loophole that in Wonderland a cat could be like a dog but Alice stops this loophole by admitting that they aren't alike, that is, it's her view of cats and dogs we are to go by.

In addition to this discussion of madness Carroll also brings out the madness contained in taking expressions, for example "mad as a March Hare," literally. Alice says, "Perhaps, as this is May it won't be raving mad—at least not so mad as it was in March." It is the case that the male hare is especially active in March as that is its rutting season. There is also a basis for the expression "mad as a hatter" it being the case that mercury used to cure felt, poisoned and affected hatters. But certainly, "mad as a March hare" and "mad as a Hatter" are loose expressions not to be taken too literally. Do not ask if a hare is literally mad in March but not in May. One is reminded of Brueghel's painting of Netherland proverbs which renders various sayings literally.

Alice, to avoid the giddiness which the cat's vanishing causes her, asks the Cat to please vanish more gradually than it had previously. The obliging Cat did so. Beginning with the end of its tail it vanished slowly until only its grin remained. The philosophical impact of this trick may be seen by comparing it with the statement that logic is pure form, devoid of content or matter. It is relevant to Plato, Aristotle, Kant and others who spoke of things like pure form and pure reason. Pure form and logic are sometimes thought of as being very much like the impossible situation of having a grin without a face.

One may also think here of what is left of a thing when all its properties are removed. Is it a metaphysical notion called substance? Is there such a thing as an invisible substance which underlies all of the qualities of a thing which one senses? Substance as an invisible entity or metaphysical category may also be like a grin without a face.

On another interpretation a grin without a face is self-contradictory. To grin is to mean that the mouth is in a certain position. (Ears do not grin.) It may be thought of as an analytic statement such as "a bachelor is an unmarried male," that is, a statement which is true by definition.

Chapter VII
A Mad Tea-Party

The question of what meaning is is then raised. Alice says, "I believe I can guess that (a riddle)."

"Do you mean that you think you can find out the answer to it?" said the March Hare.

"Exactly so," said Alice.

"Then you should say what you mean," the March Hare went on.

"I do," Alice hastily replied, "at least—at least I mean what I say—that's the same thing, you know."

"Not the same thing a bit!" said the Hatter. "Why, you might just as well say that 'I see what I eat' is the same thing as 'I eat what I see!' "

Does "I believe I can guess that," have the same meaning as that I think I can find out the answer to it? The usual picture one gets is that (1) there is a meaning or idea in one's mind separate from language which language only represents, (2) there is language, and (3) there is some sort of statement which ideas and/or words might represent. But how do we know what an idea or meaning is independent of language? Can we introspect and see them as if in a private internal theater? Think "I believe I can guess that" without words? Are there such wordless meanings or thoughts? Can one say "I believe I can guess that" and somehow internally or privately mean "I think I can find out the answer to it?" If the only solid observable evidence we have is that we speak or write language not that there are hidden processes such as thinking, having ideas, imagining, etc., going on in us somehow and somewhere, then it makes no sense to mean in one's mind one thing and say another. On this account one cannot say one thing and mean another. On this view Alice is right. "I mean what I say" is the same as "I say what I mean." The March Hare is trapping Alice in the snare of meaning difficulties.

Trivially, to "guess" something does not mean the same as to "find out" the answer to something. More than that, however, is implied here.

"I think I can find out the answer to it" is not the same sort of thing as the March Hare's saying *that* you think you can find out the answer to it. "That" here refers to some kind of statement (#3 above) other than the sentence in quotes. It is usually thought that many different sentences can represent the same statement. "Bachelors are unhappy" and "Unmarried men are unhappy" are different sentences which may be thought to represent the same statement. (On this view Alice might again be right when she says that "I say what I mean" is the same as "I mean what I say.") Instead of talking, then, about the meaning of a sentence it is thought that we can talk rather about a statement. Whether there is a statement existing in reality somewhere or somehow has, then, to be determined. But not here and now.

Less theoretically we do differentiate between "I mean what I say" and "I say what I mean." That is, we use them in different contexts. They only cause problems if we begin to look into them or try to take them literally and ask, for instance, "How do I mean what I say or say what I mean?"

The Hatter's statement that "I see what I eat" is not the same as "I eat what I see" is not clearly correct. On one interpretation one statement is the same as the other. If one does see, for example, one thing that he eats then he, as mentioned, eats that thing which he sees. On another interpretation that one sees what he eats does not imply that he eats *everything* that he sees. On this view the two statements are not the same. The Dormouse's statement that "I breathe when I sleep" is not the same as "I sleep when I breathe," is clearly true. But even here the Hatter says the two statements are nearly correct since the Dormouse is almost always sleeping. Thus each such attempt to reverse a statement needs to be examined individually to see what the meaning is. If one simply reverses any statement just because some reversed statements make sense we may say he has been misled by grammar or by the structure of our language in assuming that whatever can be grammatically constructed will yield a true statement. We are reminded of Carroll's writing a few paragraphs later, "Alice felt dreadfully puzzled. The Hatter's remark [a different one] seemed to her to have no sort of meaning in it, and yet it was certainly English." However, a good deal of insight can be gained by exploring such sentences as these. Consider:

1. I mean what I say
2. I say what I mean

1. I think what I feel
2. I feel what I think

1. I imagine what I remember
2. I remember what I imagine

By trying to decide whether these statements are the same or not we explore a possibility we may not have noticed before. We do sometimes treat "I *think* that is correct" and "I *feel* that is correct" as alternative ways of saying the same thing. Perhaps they are the same. But how do we know that they are or are not? The insight here might be that we don't know and that "I think what I feel" is just as good (or bad) as "I feel what I think." The technique of sentence reversal is especially revealing in regard to such "internal" or "mental" phenomena as these.

The riddle Alice was trying to guess, "Why is a raven like a writing-desk?" involves definition and similarities so the excursion into deciding if two statements are similar is not irrelevant. The excursion in fact may have provided the answer, although an indirect one, to the riddle. Alice tries to remember what she could about Ravens and writing desks and admits she doesn't know much about them—not enough perhaps to know why they might be similar. Our knowledge about whether meaning and saying are similar may be lacking also. Thus we may say "Is a Raven like a writing-desk?" is no more clearly answered than "Is meaning like saying?" No direct answer to the riddle is given. The Hatter says he doesn't know, in reply to Alice's request for the answer to the riddle.

Does it seem strange that one should ask a riddle without knowing the answer to it? It need not since a riddle like a question may be merely asked. We need not assume that the one who asks knows the answer nor that there even is an answer. Plato, in his dialogues, often had Socrates seek *the* definition of a term, for example, in the *Euthyphro* the definition of Piety is sought. But no definition was found satisfactory. Although Plato did not later think so, there may be no single, absolute, definition of Piety, Justice, Truth, Beauty, or of any other term. Perhaps we are misled into thinking that words, especially abstract words, name things and have a single meaning or definition. The question "What is *the* meaning of Piety?" may have no answer. There may not be an answer to every riddle or question we can ask. Many questions which philosophers and researchers ask are of this type.

The Hatter then looking at his watch as if it might have stopped asks what day of the month it is. Alice notices that the watch tells the day of the month but not what o'clock it is. There is a question as to whether we should call that a clock at all. A clock is an odd instrument in the sense that it measures change rather than time itself (if time exists). The hands of a clock move and this movement we call change of time. But it is really a change of the positions of the hands. We do not ask how long it takes for the small hand of a watch to move one hour. That is, we would never know a watch is slow if there were only one watch in existence and time is only the movement of the hands of that watch. (The standard of measure does not measure itself.) Now there is no reason why a watch should measure hours instead of days. It serves the practical purpose of meeting our needs and corresponding to change we observe, such as day and night. We can make the instrument as detailed or as crude as we wish. It could measure weeks. An hour, a minute, and a second are arbitrary units of measurement. They could be different. That depends on us and what purpose we are using them for. So why should a watch necessarily tell the hour any more than, as the Hatter suggests, a watch should tell the year? Alice replies that we don't need to tell the year by a watch because it stays the *same* year for such a long time. This situation is reflected in the question above as to how we know how long it takes for the small hand of a watch to move one hour. The Hatter replies in jest that since a watch would stay the same for a long time to measure a year, his own watch, as it seems to have stopped, would measure a long period of time too. What that period is would be as hard to determine as time would be to determine with a broken watch.

Actually the Hatter may have been confused at first about whether his watch was working or not since he would not be able to tell by glancing "every now and then" to see if it is working. It only records days of the month so he would have to wait a day to tell if it is working. That he hears it tick may tell that the wheels are working but not that the watch is correct. The hands may be stuck.

Now it seems that in attempting to fix the watch with butter the March Hare replied, "It was the *best* butter." And this is an interesting confusion. To think something is good in one circumstance tends to make us think it is good in every circumstance. Butter makes excellent pastry often but that does not mean it makes good lubrication—not even if the butter is the best. We take the best which is a superlative as having a good connotation even when it is divorced from what it modifies. Someone may tell you he will give you "the best" or "something good" on a certain occasion and you react positively without knowing what it is. It may be the best turnip. It may be the best turnip but not the best present. Or again we hear it said whatever one does one should do it well. "Be excellent at whatever you do!" But being excellent, best, or good isn't in itself enough. You may be the best murderer—thief in the world. Or we hear that one should pursue the "greatest good for the greatest number." But that does not help us determine what the "greatest good" is. Being good or the best cannot in itself be an intelligible goal. (This reminds us of Alice's earlier quandry about how to get somewhere but not knowing where she wants to go.) "Women are superior" may be flattering to them until the words ". . . to the lower animals" are added.

The notion that words are thought to name things is applied to the word "time." Alice suggests that the Hatter "might do something better with the time than wasting it in asking riddles that have no answers." To this the Hatter replies, "If you knew Time as well as I do you wouldn't talk about wasting *it*. It's *him*." The table is turned here on Alice. She objects to riddles but by talking of time as if it could be wasted she creates her own puzzles. Is time neuter? Why not a male time? To take expressions like "Can you beat time?" literally would land Alice in difficulty. The problem is similar with the term "God." What gender is God? Does God name a thing? Or is it a mistake we make to look for a thing corresponding to the word?

Now, of course, if time is a man separate from clocks we have a confusion. We no longer know what time is. There is no standard to measure it, to know that it is there, much less male. But that is just it, we never knew that it was an it rather than a him. Time need not be a thing and there need not exist simple absolute time or time which leaps or time which passes from future to present to past neatly packaged as minutes and seconds. There need not be time in itself at all.

Alice disclaims that if Time could change time "in a twinkling" to 1:30, her lunchtime, then she might not yet be hungry. What is odd here is:

1. the ability of time to change itself

2. the ability of time to change suddenly. For what would suddenly mean here?

3. the relationship between time and objects. Can time alone cause one to be hungry? If time is changed to 1:30 suddenly are objects also changed? Can time exist independent of objects such that it can change without objects changing? Suppose that time changed from 9:30 to 1:30 but nothing else changed. We would never know that time so changed and it would make no difference to anyone. 1:30 would still be treated as 9:30 and four hours later Alice would eat as usual.

We see that expressions we ordinarily use in regard to time make little sense if taken literally. The Queen of Hearts says, "He's murdering time!" which, although it sounds strange, could easily be a reference to our everyday expression, "killing time." The Hatter says that since he "killed time" by singing at someone else's (the Queen of Hearts') concert, Time "won't do a thing I ask! It's [He's] always six o'clock now." What could that mean? The situation is the same as above where time suddenly changed to 1:30. That is, everything will go on even though time, whether it is independent of objects, stops or not. What would affect things is if objects no longer changed.

Because six o'clock is tea time and time has stopped, the Hatter mistakenly thinks what is done at that time must stop also. That is, he sets a table with many places supposing that he must have tea over and over as time stopped at tea time. This is not unlike some of Zeno's paradoxes which confuse time with what takes place in time or which assume that time is something separate from the change of things or events.

One would think that if time stopped at 6:00 and if time is just change of objects, that then at 6:00 nothing would move. But that is not the case. The Hatter keeps having tea in what he calls "whiles." Tea time would be such a "while" or duration and if time stopped here we would have duration left and change taking place in that duration. This is contradictory to the view that time is change. It suggests that time stops yet goes on; that change stops, yet goes on. Questions are suggested as to whether time should be thought of in terms of objects or objects in terms of time; whether we should talk about time in terms of physical terminology or vice versa. Nearly every philosopher has had some say about the nature of time. The notion of duration just raised suggests Bergson's view that time cannot be reduced to space. There are no spatial times only living tea times.

After the Hatter explained to Alice why he was condemned (or rather condemned himself) to have one tea time over and over by going from tea cup to tea cup around the table Alice asks "But what happens when you come to the beginning again?" The meaninglessness of repeating a moment which is never the same, of identifying having tea with an independent and ideal sort of time, and of reaching a beginning when time no longer "passes" lead the March Hare to change the subject. The motif of the riddle is thus continued. We say things we can't explain. Some ordinary seeming statements and expressions turn out to be useless and meaningless if taken literally. So the subject is changed indicating, perhaps, that there is no answer. Or the answer is the March Hare's saying, "Suppose we change the subject. I'm getting tired of this. I vote the young lady tells us a story." We are misled by thinking that words name things and by confusing different contexts. "Time passes" is not like "A train passes." And it is seen that just what time is is somewhat of a paradox. One solution of the paradox might be that time as an entity in itself does not exist. "Time," "minute," "year," etc., do not name things. All we can observe is clock hands changing position, day and night, change of planetary positions, or change or movement of objects (and possibly psychological change). But we do not observe time. Another solution might be that time means something but not one thing. What time and time words mean depends on their use. "Have a good time" means only "Have fun" and does not refer to or name or describe time. "We have one minute to go," does not name or describe or refer to a thing called a "minute." Rather we learn to utter "minute" in a certain situation and so "minute" has as many meanings as it has uses in different contexts. It does not name or refer to something called "time." Another way of saying this is there is no one definition or essence of time. To find out what time is, then, we would merely look and see how time words are used in our everyday language. The examples given above, "Have a good time" and "He was killing time," indicate such usage. "By the time" the end of the chapter "comes" and Carroll writes "*then* she. . . till. . . :*then* she. . . : and *then*. . . " we become very conscious of those time words we usually take for granted.

The March Hare invites Alice to "take some more tea." Alice objects to this invitation saying "I've had nothing yet so I can't take more." The Hatter adds, "You mean you can't take *less*, it's very easy to take *more* than nothing." Certainly if one hasn't had any he can't take more. Too much is assumed. It is not unlike "Have you stopped beating your children?" when you have no children and did not beat them. But we do assume too much in many of our ordinary assertions.

The statement "You mean you can't take *less*, it's very easy to take *more* than nothing," assumes that "nothing" names a thing which one has had. But "nothing" does not name a thing. Philosophers sometimes use the word as if it does name a thing. Parmenides says that what is inside the sphere of Being is and what is outside is nothing and is nameless. If it is nameless it seems odd that Parmenides can still refer to it as nothing. Furthermore there is a question as to what nothing means where something can never be. There is nothing here might only make sense where there is something here, does make sense. To say there is nothing where something can never be is odd. There is much controversy about what words such as "not" and "no" and what negative statements refer to. If "anger" in "I am angry" refers to an emotion what emotion does "not angry" in "I am not angry" refer to? The way out of the difficulty might be to see that neither "anger" nor "not angry" refer to anything in us at all but rather to external, intersubjective behavioral and linguistic phenomena.

Carroll's puns should not be overlooked. The Dormouse tells a story of three sisters who were *ill*, living in a *well*. They were in the well, "*well*" in. When the March Hare put butter in the watch with a bread-knife, the Hatter supposes that some bread must have gotten in the watch. By this same reasoning if one uses a fish knife some fish would have gotten in. Ambiguity of reference is also capitalized on. Alice says "Nobody asked *your* opinion," to which the Hatter responds with "who's making personal remarks now?" The Hatter could mean Alice here but since he has just assumed that nothing is a thing he could well mean that Nobody also is making personal remarks. Such ambiguity adds force to the exposition of confusions which trap us in our thinking as we use language. We, for instance, often have the idea that the etymology of a word determines what its meaning really is. "Philosophy" means in Greek, "love of wisdom" but as a definition or a use of the word philosophy we may be quite misled by this—just as much as thinking that one can't get ill in a well. Philosophy might not be just love.

The well is supposedly a treacle-well (molasses-well) and one would assume that since one draws water from a water well, one could draw treacle from a treacle well. This is pointed out by the Hatter. And this is another way in which language can mislead us. Because there is faculty psychology does not mean that there is student psychology. One does not wake flowers out of a flower bed.

Now a rather deep problem is raised. (Well, it might well be as *deep* as the treacle-well.) The three sisters were drawing all kinds of things beginning with the letter "M." But could they draw *all* kinds? The Dormouse says they draw "mouse-traps, and the moon, and memory, and muchness—you know you say things are 'much of a muchness'—did you ever see such a thing as a drawing of a muchness?" Muchness is obviously incorrectly regarded here as a thing instead of a modifier. Consider the question "What would you like?" and the answer "A lot." It is thought that a lot, in itself, is better than a little and that is not necessarily so. Not being a thing "much" cannot be drawn (much less drawn from a well). Neither can we draw memory. To this we may add that neither our internal states nor objects such as invisible ghosts or God can be drawn. But why would one want to draw them? Perhaps because they think that some thing, image or picture must correspond to each word uttered. But we see that we cannot draw "memory," "mind," or "muchness." It is odd too to try to draw everything beginning with "M" because things do not begin with letters, words do. The question of how a thing is related to its name is raised here.

In reply to the question whether she saw a drawing of muchness, Alice replied, "Really, now you ask me I don't think ——." To this the Hatter says, "Then you shouldn't talk." We are back to the notion of negation here. If you know what you do when you do think, what do you do when you don't think? The issue here also is that our expressions are odd if taken literally. In addition the model of thinking as supposedly being needed as causing or accompanying talking blends in with the two issues just mentioned. We cannot draw thought or mind. What evidence do we have that it is there? But where? And is it an "it"? Suppose Alice did speak without there being some supposedly hidden process, as thought is thought to be. Would that make any difference to anyone? It adds nothing to say "My mind or thought caused it to be said," rather than "I said it." Carroll seems to suggest that what thought is and, if it is anything, how it relates to language is not at all clear. The problem may be so deep because we are misled into looking for entities where there are none, and asking improper or meaningless questions.

Chapter VIII
The Queen's Croquet-Ground

Here Carroll gives us some lessons in justice and how to perform it (or play it). The characters are the various playing cards such as the Deuce, Five, Seven, King and Queen of Hearts, clubs, Jack of Hearts (called a Knave of Hearts here) etc. The Queen has one solution for every difficulty that arises—"cut off their heads." We are reminded of the present day practice in various countries of getting rid of political opposition; and of giving the same sort of verdict for nearly any crime: imprisonment. It is not always clear how such imprisonment is supposed to rehabilitate the offender. It may make him more of a criminal. Some emphasis is, however, now being placed on correction rather than sheer punishment. War also seems to be a universal cure-all for one's difficulties. Certainly one cannot help think of the frequent beheadings we (and Alice) read about in history as the Queen repeats over and over "Off with their heads."

The next lesson is that to remove a head is not correctional justice. What can one learn if he has been executed? The Queen says that the card Seven deserves to be beheaded and when Two asks why, Seven says "That's none of *your* business." We may note that the cards are related since two plus five equals seven. This relation might suggest social dependence and so what is the business of one is the business of the other. Later the Queen sees three cards which she cannot identify because they are face down and reveal only their backs which have the same pattern as all of the cards do. She asks, "And who are *these*?" to which Alice, pretending not to know, says, "How should I know? It's no business of *mine*." But responsibility and justice is not something we possess as we possess a coat. Moral and ethical actions are everyone's concern. They are about relationships between people and involve everyone. It is the living who must learn about what is right and wrong and help others to learn also. It's everyone's business.

The Queen's metering out of justice is nothing new to us, as we indicated, but it is soon seen how inappropriate it is to the various occasions. She orders the heads of several cards be cut off—but cards have no heads. She orders Alice's head off but the King intercedes saying, "Consider, my dear: she is only a child!" She orders the Cat's head off but the Cat has only a head, the rest of its body not having appeared. The question then arises as to how a bodiless head could be beheaded. It can't. It is an inappropriate command. The Queen then asserts that if they don't decide fast about beheading the Cat *everyone* there will be executed. This too is inappropriate in the sense that not *all* can be executed. If all were, then the Queen would be executed and even the executioner would have to cut his own head off. Carroll suggests in this way that there is no one-shot solution to problems of justice.

Now in this fine art of cutting heads off we see that the Queen is giving an order. What she says is law or a rule of justice to be carried out. But we see next how difficult it sometimes is to apply rules. We can not know in all possible situations how a rule should be applied. The soldiers are commissioned to cut off the heads of the three cards, Two, Five, and Seven but the three cards are out of sight. The soldiers return to the Queen who asks, "Are their heads off?" The soldiers report, "their heads are gone, if it please your Majesty." Those persons concerned to cut off someone's head were so centered about the mechanical difficulties involved that they lost sight of the reason why it was being done. Isn't it enough that the Cat fade away and the three cards disappear?

The Queen uses "Cut off their heads" so much that it is not certain that she means anything by it. Perhaps it functions merely like an emotional outburst and it's true that justice is often metered out that way. One may repeat a word, slogan or phrase so much that it loses its meaning. And that might show that the meaning of words depends on situations and contexts. (The Queen says when the soldiers report that the heads of the three cards are gone, "that's right." "Right" here is a pun meaning both "that's fine" and "that is what right is.") We may desire therefore to reexamine our laws from time to time as well as their specific applications.

The importance of the use of the language of justice is again suggested by the pun on Knave. Knave is a Jack in cards and is also a deceitful fellow. We see that words may be charged with emotion by calling someone a Knave instead of a

Jack and so also we accuse people of being such things as communists, etc., on the basis of some insignificant quality which they might possess.

Another aspect of justice is tradition. People, for example, cut off heads because they have always done so. Alice says about the Queen's procession that although the three cards are lying face down she does not see why she should "and besides, what would be the use of a procession if people had to lie down on their faces, so that they couldn't see it?" But many formalities and traditions aren't meant to be practical, pragmatic, intelligible, or even observed. The Queen's servants may obey her because they always have done so as well as to avoid getting their heads chopped off.

So justice may not consist merely of a sort of rule or command one can blanketly follow. It may be more like the Queen's Croquet Game in which the mallets are flamingoes, the croquet balls live hedgehogs, and the soldiers double up to make arches. There seem to be no absolute rules for the game or at least, as Alice says, either they are hard to find or no one attends to them. We find enough contradictions and difficulties in attempting to determine what justice is to give some support to this. Some say that law is what will get to be decided in the courtroom. Others say law is determined almost solely by the existing laws. We see that rules of church and state often conflict. We have difficulty in determining how to execute laws and rules. We see how large a factor language plays in determining whether a man's behavior is accurately and consistently described and so whether he is to be found guilty or not guilty.

Chapter IX
The Mock Turtle's Story

Alice begins a statement with "When I'm a Duchess. . . " which, since she doesn't know that she will be one, would be better phrased "If I become a Duchess. . . " She imagines that perhaps various foods, such as sugar, have specific effects on character, such as making one sweet. One's language suggests a closeness of the statements (a) Sugar is sweet and (b) Her disposition is sweet. The parallel is misleading if it is only based upon taking "sweet" in the second statement literally. That a specific food causes a specific character trait such as "hot-temper" is questionable, whether that food is hot peppered soup or not. Charles Lamb, the nineteenth century English essayist, asserts that asparagus gives one pleasant thoughts. If a specific food has a specific effect on such character traits what food must a person eat to be "nice" rather than "cordial?" Would peas do for "nice" and "peas with butter" for "cordial?"

The Duchess says to Alice "You're thinking about something, my dear, and that makes you forget to talk." This statement suggests that one may not be able to think and talk at the same time. If there is such a process as thinking$_1$ going on and if we also have to think$_2$ to put our thoughts$_1$ in words then perhaps we can't think$_1$ and think$_2$ at the same time. This may show the limitations of the notion of thinking. Perhaps we speak and speech is thought, there being no separate process to call thought. Similar to the Duchess' statement is the idea that we do not know of our having a consciousness because we can never catch ourselves thinking. If one is thinking$_1$ and to have consciousness is to think$_2$ (or be aware) of thinking$_1$ then since we may never be thinking$_2$ while thinking$_1$ we may conclude that we do not know what consciousness is in this sense.

The Duchess' statement also raises the problem of other minds. How does the Duchess know that Alice is thinking if Alice isn't speaking, but also how does anyone know what thinking is at all? Later in the chapter the Duchess asks, "Thinking again?" Alice replies "I've a right to think." "Just about as much right as pigs have to fly," the Duchess concludes. But it may not be a matter of right in regard to thought. One may have a right to draw a round square or multiply two and three to get blue but still not know how or be able to do it. One may in this sense have no more right to think one is thinking than a pig has to fly.

As the Queen had one solution for every difficulty, decapitation, the Duchess held there must be a moral to everything: "Everything's got a moral, if only you can find it." Presumably even this statement has a moral. The statement is a bit ironical because as the Duchess utters it she rudely digs her sharp chin into Alice's shoulder. It is wrong in another way to say that every story *has* a moral. No story *has* a moral but one can always find or put one there. The Duchess can never be wrong and this is why Alice's statement, "Perhaps it hasn't one (a moral)," is questionable.

Sentences are sometimes categorized as descriptive or non-descriptive with ethical terms falling in the latter group. To say "This table is red" is to report that the quality, red, applies to the table but to say "This table is good" does not attribute a quality to the table. About any descriptive statement one may ask, "Is it good?" If one says, for example, "The chair is red" it may also be asked if it is good. To say that everything has a moral, and not just whether every story has a moral, is to say that we can ask the further question, "Is it good?," "Is it right?," "Should that be?" etc. A moral is a lesson serving as a reply to this sort of question, often referred to as a normative as opposed to a scientific question.

The moral the Duchess finds for Alice's statement, "The game's [the Queen's Croquet game] going on rather better now," is "Oh, 'tis love, 'tis love that makes the world go round!" What is indicated here is the abstractness with which behavioral and causal situations are described. It is implied that this is a moral statement because one *should* love one's neighbor so that the game will go right. There is irony here, of course, because of the Queen's apparent cruelty during the game. The moral could be "Hate or aggression makes the world go around," were it not also too abstract to be true or false. If one maintains that "It's love that mkes the world go round" he may be committed to holding that love makes all of the harmful, hateful things happen also. Moral statements of this sort are examples of one-shot solutions to problems just as is the Queen's method of decapitation. Perhaps Carroll is hinting that the majority of books written on history and human behavior consist primarily of statements of the above normative or abstract sort.

The second moral given, this time by Alice, is "Somebody said that it's [the going around of the world or the success of the croquet game] done by everybody minding their own business." This also is a slogan as is "It's love that makes the world go round." The Duchess says that these two statements mean much the same thing. That is, both statements may be alike in being devoid of any clear or justifiable meaning. On another view, the two statements may mean the same thing because love may be defined as minding one's own business. This is such a negative definition that it is humorous. Nevertheless, laissez-faire philosophies are often based on it.

The moral of the statement that the two statements mean much the same thing is, "Take care of the sense and the sounds will take care of themselves," a play on the phrase "Take care of the pence and the pounds will take care of themselves." This again is a questionable slogan as Carroll no doubt realizes. What is the relation between the meaning of a word and the letters and sounds which they supposedly "represent?" How do we take care of the sense (the meaning)? The question is dealt with throughout Carroll's writings. The issue here is mainly whether two different sentences can have identical meaning. It is often held by logicians that the statement can be the same even though the sentences, words, and sounds are different. On the other hand if there are no meanings or facts separate from observable linguistic behavior two different sentences might never be the same. Certainly the connotations of two different sentences cannot be the same. It would not make sense to substitute something like "mind one's business" wherever "love" appears. "I love you" would become "I mind my business." Because the definition of love cannot be intelligibly substituted for "love" in nearly any of its many uses it is doubtful that they mean the same except by arbitrary definition. But by arbitrary definition kangaroos can be defined as being identical with foxes and 3 + 4 can be defined as equal to eleven.

The next lesson Carroll teaches us is similar to the previous. We should not take slogans too literally or seriously but neither should we do the same with categories. The Duchess asserts that flamingoes and mustard both bite and the moral is "Birds of a feather flock together." Alice is still carrying the flamingo which she acquired in the croquet game. She replies that mustard isn't a bird and that she thinks it is a mineral. The confusion is simple. Alice is trying to put everything into the three categories of animal, mineral, or vegetable. Mustard might seem more appropriate to the category of mineral than that of vegetable because of its immediate appearance. In the broad sense anything may be classified as a vegetable which comes from a plant. In the narrow and common sense vegetable refers to only the edible part of a herbaceous plant. There is frequently a difficulty of classification because it is not always clear what the purpose of the classification is and the categories are often inadequate in regard to clarity or number.

Philosophers have attempted to reduce sentences to categories in a similarly procrustean manner. On one view a statement is either analytic such as "All bachelors are unmarried" or synthetic such as "The chair is green." On another view a sentence is either descriptive, such as "The chair is green" or emotive such as "He is a *good* person." (Ethical statements are sometimes thought to be as emotive as saying "ouch.")

The Duchess replies to Alice's statement, "Mustard isn't a bird," with "Right, as usual. What a clear way you have of putting things." It does seem clear for certain purposes that mustard and flamingoes are not in the same categories. They are not birds. But for other purposes they can be put in the same class. They do both bite, the bird with its beak and mustard bites (stings) the tongue. Alice does have a clear way of putting things in the sense that she doesn't put things in any way at all but merely excludes mustard from the category, bird. But her clarity here is not carried over to her categorization of mustard as a mineral. Categories are not always what they seem. She does finally state, "It's a vegetable. It doesn't look like one, but it is."

The Duchess says the moral of the last statement above is " 'Be what you would seem to be'—or, if you'd like it put more simply—'Never imagine yourself not to be otherwise than what it might appear to others that what you were or might have been was not otherwise than what you had been would have appeared to them to be otherwise.' " To this Alice replies, "I think I should understand that better if I had it written down: but I ca'n't quite follow it as you say it." This statement is especially meaningful if compared with the earlier one, "Take care of the sense and the sounds will take care of themselves." It would seem that perhaps now Alice needs more than sense to grasp what the Duchess' words say. She needs to see the words, write them down. And further it is not clear that "Be what you would seem to be" is equivalent to the long statement which follows it. This is not to say there is not some similarity. It is questionable whether the long restatement ever has use in ordinary language. Consequently it may have meaning only as it may be derived from sentences which are more simple and have ordinary use. Part of the meaning of the restated statement would have to be "I am trying to unduly complicate matters" and in this sense has at least one intelligible use. We need not think that every set of grammatical sentences has a clear use or meaning. Carroll offers us an interesting challenge here to try to find one, one identical with "Be what you would seem to be." Whether we find it or not we see the irony of a sentence being what it seems to be.

We earlier saw that various slogans and sayings are not as true as they seem. A strange animal called a Gryphon is introduced. The Gryphon is not what he seems to us as the more common name is griffin, that is, an animal which is half-bird and half-lion. Carroll writes, " 'What fun!' said the Gryphon, half to itself, half to Alice." This sentence is not quite what it seems, either, because of its several puns. Fun refers to the second part of the name Gry - *phon* and half to itself, half to Alice and it has connotations of its being half one kind of animal and half another. The Gryphon seems to believe in appearance not reality when it says about the Queen "It's all her fancy that: they never executes nobody," and about the Mock Turtle, "It's all his fancy, that: he hasn't got no sorrow." In the case of the Queen if she is a card she can't execute anyone. The King pardoned everyone she condemned. The deck was reshuffled, so to speak, in a game of cards. It just seemed like a real happening. As for the Mock Turtle, he has no sorrow because he isn't real, but mock. The recipe for Mock Turtle Soup is: Calf's head, veal, other meat and condiments in imitation of Green Turtle Soup. And so there is no such thing as a Mock Turtle, and so no sorrow. The Gryphon's two statements above have a double negative in them which also makes things appear to be what they are not.

The main theme of the chapter is now evident. The examples so far have revolved around the question of appearance and reality. Are things what they seem to be? The chapter begins with the Duchess saying "You ca'n't think how glad I am. . . " This is the clue from the start since "ca'n't" might really refer to Kant who separated phenomena from noumena,[2] appearance from reality. In many ways things are not what they seem to be and Carroll has given us a few instances. In the discussion of the categories animal, vegetable, and mineral we are reminded of Kant's categories which legislate for experience. That is, Kant held that all experience is "seen through" certain categories such as space, time, cause-effect, substance-accident, etc. The Duchess' assertion that everything has a moral if only one can find it may be related to Kant's notion that everyone has a duty which he must obey, if only he can find it. That there is mustard suggests to the Duchess that there is a mustard-machine, reminds us of Kant's faculty psychology. That is, where there is a function there must be a faculty responsible for it. It is even remotely possible to take the moral "The more there is of mine, the less there is of yours," as "The more there is of *mind,* the less one knows one's self." The Kantian stress on mind is also emphasized by Alice's being told several times that she is "thinking again." " 'I've a right to think,' Alice says," is very much like Kant's *synthetic a priori* (that which exists before

---

[2] noumena—that which we cannot know yet which is real in itself. We can only know appearances. "Ca'n't" may also be used to mark the missing letters from "cannot."

experience yet applies to experience). Kant says that the mind legislates or partly contributes to the way in which we view reality and so gives us a "right to think." Alice's statement, "I don't see how he can *ever* finish, if he doesn't begin" reminds us of Kant's first antinomy the thesis involving "The world has a beginning in time" and the antithesis, "The world has no beginning, and. . . is infinite as regards. . . time. . . " Alice's statement, "There *must* be more to come" suggests Kant's categorical imperative. The Mock Turtle's statement, "Well, I ca'n't show it you, myself," would be a precise statement of the inaccessibility of reality in itself (noumena). The Mock Turtle's added comment that he can't faint in coils because he is "too stiff" might suggest that Kant's categories do not allow us to see reality directly or that our own categories don't. The Gryphon then says, "Hadn't time [to learn]" and time is one of the central Kantian categories. Alice legislates in Kantian fashion when she says that she thinks certain foods (e.g. pepper) make people have certain traits (hot-temper) and that she only wishes that people (or everyone) knew that. The Duchess' statement "You're thinking about something, my dear, and that makes you forget to talk," may suggest Kant's notion that form and matter are both needed for experience—both sense impressions and categories. The Duchess' identification of love and minding one's own business could be an expression of the Kantian maxim that one should oneself so act (minding one's business) that one would will that act be universalized (involving others suggesting a form of concern or love). The often repeated words "Come on!" may suggest the Kantian notion of duty and the categorical imperative.

Even the definition of Mock Turtle seems to be a definition but isn't one. Alice says, "I don't even know what a Mock Turtle is." The Queen replies, "It's the thing Mock Turtle Soup is made from." This, if a definition at all, is a circular one. It tells nothing about what a Mock Turtle is. And Mock Turtle is only the name of a soup.

Chapter X
The Lobster-Quadrille

After some fun, puns, and dancing the Mock Turtle says, "No wise fish would go anywhere without a porpoise."[3] Alice objects, "Don't you mean 'purpose?' " "I mean what I say," the Mock Turtle replies, renewing the question of whether one can mean something different than what one says. If Wittgenstein's theory of meaning is correct, that the meaning of a word is its use in an ordinary situation, then the meaning of Wittgenstein's own statements have meaning only as *they* are used in a certain situation. That is, what Wittgenstein means is what he says. Any term, such as "explanation," depends for its meaning on its use in a

---

[3] Because it may bring one luck to do so.

context. Its purpose need not be to describe or explain. "Explanation" may be of no higher level than the word "chair." Both depend on the utterance of the word in the right situation and in the right linguistic context.

The conversation continues on and Alice tries to recite a poem. The poem has the esoteric title, "The voice of the sluggard." But what is the purpose of reciting poems? Does it help one understand? If not, the moral "No wise fish would go anywhere without a porpoise," would apply. Carroll does attack education in a way which extends beyond Alice's preoccupations and frustrations with it. In the previous chapter the Mock Turtle puns on his teacher who was called "Tortoise" because he "taught us." There is a pun on lessons which *lessen* by one hour every day that being why they are called lessons. In addition such subjects are taught as Uglification (multiplication), Ambition (addition), Reeling (reading), Writhing (writing), Distraction (subtraction), Derision (division), Mystery (history), Drawling (drawing), Stretching (sketching), Laughing and Grief (Latin and Greek), Seaography (geography), and Fainting in Coils (painting in oils). In this chapter (X) the question as to what an explanation is is raised and this issue is quite relevant to education also. If we do not want education to be mere repetition then should it consist of explanations? But what are they?

The Mock Turtle asks Alice, "What is the use of repeating all that stuff [the second verse of the poem] if you don't explain it as you go on?" Earlier Alice says, "I could tell you my adventures—beginning from this morning but it's no use going back to yesterday, because I was a different person then." To this the Mock Turtle responds, "Explain all that," and the Gryphon protests saying "Explanations take such a dreadful time." Concerning the first verse of Alice's rendering of the poem the Mock Turtle says, "I should like to have it explained." "She ca'n't explain it," the Gryphon suggests. The reference here to Kant may be significant.

The notion of explanation played a part earlier as when the Caterpillar asks Alice to explain herself, as a general directive. That is, it is not clear what sort of answer is desired. She can't (Kant) explain it. What appears to be an explanation falls short, but short of what? The Kantian noumenal (real, in itself) situation? Is there an explanation to exhaust all further inquiry—a noumenal explanation? The pragmatists take explanation as the pacification of doubt. If an explanation removes one's disturbance caused by doubt then it is a meaningful or true explanation. Whether or not this is an adequate view of truth or meaning it is close to the ordinary notion of explanation which is giving an answer which satisfies. One may give a logical explanation in terms of non-contradiction or definitions; or an epistemological explanation in terms of how we know such and such is the case; or ontological explanations in terms of what something consists of. But there is an infinite number of types of explanation. In the next chapter Alice, who has never been in a courtroom before, says, "That's the judge, *because* of his great wig." (My italics.) One may see here a modification of or exception to Kant's notion that we must think of things in terms of cause and effect relations. "Because" is nearly always a difficult notion to cope with. When it is not clear what sort of explanation is wanted, confusion results. One may not know where to stop explaining. For the explanation of one's address one may put: I, John Smith, House #23, Main St., Avon, Rye County, Connecticut, U.S.A., The World, The Universe, and write an account to attempt to specify the rest. But with each new explanation ignorance is put off just one step.

Explanations are sometimes reasons, causes, or excuses. Consider the explanation for one's going to a play. One may give the following:
 (a) I had not seen it before.
 (b) I was bored.
 (c) I had nothing to keep me here.
 (d) I just felt like it.
 (e) I don't know why, I just went.
 (f) The physiological constitution of my body was such that I was determined to go.
 (g) Why shouldn't I have gone?
 (h) etc.

It does not make sense to ask which of these is correct. Correctness has to do with a purpose (Porpoise). Most, if not all of them, are socially acceptable and in this respect constitute acceptable explanations. None of them may be correct in the sense of being completely intelligible. If one asserts that he went because he was bored one can still ask whether boredom is a proper cause. Do not say my will caused me to do a certain act unless there is such a thing as a will and we can describe what it is like. To speak of the will is reminiscent of the outdated and unintelligible faculty psychology. Does anyone know oneself well enough to know what really caused him to do a certain act? This would be an especially significant question for those who, like Freudians, maintain that motivation takes place primarily on the unconscious level.

The phrase "Explain yourself," reminds one of Socrates' "Know yourself." Socrates answer was that he knew he knew nothing. For the philosopher, Wittgenstein, "explanation" is a word we use and react to in everyday experience and is of no different or higher level than "chair." "Explanations" do not on this view explain anymore than does "table." The words are merely used. (For a further account of this view it would be necessary to read at least Wittgenstein's *Philosophical Investigations*.) The account Carroll suggests in regard to explanation and its relation, for example, to Kant supports the theme of the previous chapter—that things are not always what they seem.

An important side issue is raised at the end of this chapter when the Mock Turtle sings "Beautiful Soup, so rich and green. / Soup of the evening, Beautiful, beautiful Soup!" Now we do not as a rule refer to soup as being beautiful anymore than we say, "Have you seen the beautiful weeds in my back yard?" Weeds and soup are interesting in that respect. Soup is meant to be eaten and so is more properly delicious than beautiful. There is no reason, of course, why an artist should not make a soup just for looks. Weeds, however, seems to include one's value judgment from the start. We call a plant a weed because it is unwanted. In one sense then "a beautiful (wanted) weed" is a contradiction. As it happens, though, some weeds are more attractive than some flowers. The same sort of combination as "beautiful soup" can be applied to ethics as, for instance, in "good criminal" or "desirable pain." Carroll's combination of beautiful with soup may be further explored in this direction.

By writing beautiful soup as "Beau–ootiful Soo-op!" and "beauti-FUL SOUP!" Carroll calls attention to the singing of the words as if the words were quite important and meaningful. When words are sung they often are not important much less understood. But even when they are significant there is a question as to what is added to their meaning by singing them. Carroll is exploring these relationships between the spoken word and the word which is sung.

Chapter XI
Who Stole the Tarts?

The title of this chapter may well be what it seems, that is, a lesson in law. The king, to begin with, has a crown on his wig which looks uncomfortable. This may be a subtle way of suggesting that justice and the law should not rest solely in the hands of the king. But there are other ways in which justice may be obstructed, or not be as objective and as equitable as it might seem. Alice is proud that she knows the meaning of such technical words as "jurors," whereas as Carroll points out "jurymen" would have done just as well. The suggestion is that possible legal language may be needlessly technical and inaccessible to the average person (not just to little girls). "Jurors" certainly sounds like an official enough body but their function in a courtroom is questionable. Are they, being average citizens, qualified to understand such technical terms as lawyers use, so as to deliver a correct verdict? The jurors begin writing before the trial begins and Alice says, "They ca'n't have anything to put down yet, before the trial's begun." The Gryphon replies, "They're putting down their names for fear they should forget them before the end of the trial." "Stupid things," Alice said and the jurors wrote down "Stupid things" in their notes, one of them not knowing how to spell "stupid." The jury might be thought of as taking down, as they actually do here, three different dates of a single event, summing up the dates and reducing the sum to shillings and pence. Also the concept of a jury being composed of a number of people such that truth will be determined by the majority may be democratic but it is strange as a criterion of truth. Truth is not voted into existence or determined by the majority of relatively uninformed opinions. In the next chapter there is a general clapping of hands at a statement the King makes and the Queen concludes from such applause, "That *proves* his guilt, of course, so off with—[his head]."

Alice's statement that they "ca'n't (Kant) have anything to put down yet" suggests that they have a great deal to put down. It appears that although the trial begins in the courtroom, each person brings his own previously determined values to bear on the judgment. Such values are not usually made evident or discussed openly. One's regional, religious, or political views may for instance affect the verdict regardless of evidence presented or of being aware that one is being swayed by such values. Kant is relevant here in terms of his notion of the *a priori,* that the mind contributes its own categories to the constitution of reality. Here the jurors bring with them their own *a priori* categories. It is often these values that are appealed to to sway the decisions of the jurors. (Kant employed much legal terminology in showing how the mind legislates experience. He distinguishes between "judgments of fact" and "judgments of right." He spoke of how we should "police" the human understanding in order to see what its limitations are. For Kant of duty and categorical imperative function as laws which should be obeyed. Kant, as lawyers do, used a great number of technical, and supposedly careful, terms. Kant's interpreters have tried ever since he wrote his Critiques to render his terms more clear or intelligible. We may also note the coincidence, if it wasn't intended, that there are twelve jurors and that Kant has twelve main categories.)

The King tells the Hatter "Don't be nervous, or I'll have you executed on the spot." Alice finds she is suddenly growing fast and the Dormouse says, "You've no right to grow *here.*" And the King addressing the Hatter says, "You *must* remember or I'll have you executed." These are not the sorts of things one can legislate about as one supposedly does not have control of them. And the question is raised as to what one can legislate about. Are our actions free or determined by prior causes? If they are determined and we were not therefore able to do otherwise than we did, we should neither be blamed or praised for them. Clarence Darrow often offered a successful defense on the grounds that the past environment of his client had been such that the latter could not help but do the act. We may have no right to obey or not obey the law of gravity. It applies to us whether we want it to or not. Kant made the distinction between laws and maxims. A law we can act according to without knowing it but a maxim is a rule or law we choose to act from. "Right" should not apply to what is beyond our control. Carroll may be suggesting that there are areas where we are accused for things which are beyond our control. Controversial questions of law may be raised along these lines.

A lesson suggested in Chapter Nine would be appropriate here. The King pardons those ordered to be executed and Alice is relieved because she had begun to be uneasy at so many people being executed. But it is odd to be uneasy because of the number being unjustly executed. (It is questionable whether anyone can be *justly* executed.) If killing is wrong in one instance, it should be just as wrong as if ten people are unjustly killed. From this point of view it is just as wrong to kill one person as to drop a bomb on a city thereby killing thousands. Yet it is seen that injustice is often thought not to be done, especially in regard to international affairs, unless large numbers perish. The question raised is "When does an issue become a moral issue?"

We saw earlier that Alice was asked to explain herself. One way of explaining oneself is to give evidence as to what one had been doing at certain times. This sort of explanation is often required in a courtroom. What was said earlier about explanation of one's behavior applies all the more in a courtroom. Was one's action premeditated? How can this be accurately determined? Perhaps one just did it without thinking but it looked from the external evidence as if it were premeditated. Did the accused intend to do the action? If so, what is the nature of an intention? Is an intention running the whole act over in one's mind before it happens? Should one be blamed for bad intentions even when they are not carried out? Alice is next asked to give evidence in her own behalf.

Chapter XII
Alice's Evidence

Alice is called on to testify or give evidence and, having forgotten how large she has just become, jumps up too quickly thereby upsetting the jury-box. She exclaims, "Oh, I *beg* your pardon." This is a legal pun if the expression is taken literally—a request to be pardoned. More interesting, however, is the fact that "I beg your pardon," is inappropriate to such an act as upsetting a jury-box. John Austin in "A Plea for Excuses"[4] writes, "We may plead that we trod on the snail inadvertently: but not on a baby—you ought to look where you're putting your great feet." Stepping on a baby is too grave for which to accept an excuse or pardon. The standards of acceptance of an excuse are different with different acts. A wrong spelling may be a slip but not an accident. "Pardon me" is unacceptable when one knocks over an entire jury-box or if one throws a grenade in a crowd. In a courtroom especially we should be alert to which acts are called inadvertent, mistakes, negligent, slips, accidents, etc. Austin presents an actual court case, *Regina v. Finney*, in which faulty and inappropriate descriptions are given. Austin writes about this case, "Both counsel and judge

---

[4] John Austin, "A Plea for Excuses," *Essays in Philosophical Psychology,* ed. D. Gustafson, (New York: Doubleday, 1964) pp. 1-29.

make very free use of a large number of terms of excuse, using several as though they were, and even stating them to be indifferent or equivalent when they are not, and presenting as alternatives those that are not."

The determination of whether an act is to be called "inadvertent," "negligent" or "accidental" reminds us of the King's saying "important-unimportant-unimportant-important" to see which sounds best as a test of which word he means. Can we go just by the sound as we sometimes seem to?

Austin points out that we should pay attention to the opposite of a term and try to determine if (a) it has an opposite and (b) what it means to be opposite. We say "unimportant-important" but not "inadvertent-advertent." The prefix im- and in- does not always negate the word prefixed. What should be taken then as the opposite of "inadvertent?" Would it be "attentive," "intentional," or "on purpose?" The difference between these terms can be significant when accuracy is needed.

What would the opposite of a term be? What is the opposite of the term "yellow" (other than the color physically opposite it on a color chart)? The notion of excluded middle or either-or type of thinking is touched on by Carroll when in the previous chapter the King says to the Hatter, "Take off your hat," the Hatter replies, "It isn't mine." The King then assumes that the hat must be stolen. But the opposite of its not being my hat need not be that it is stolen. It may be borrowed or it may be being displayed for a fee or one may simply be selling the hat (which is the Hatter's case).

In the present chapter, the King says to the prisoner, the Knave, "If you didn't sign it (a letter whose authorship is uncertain) that only makes the matter worse. You *must* have meant some mischief or else you'd have signed your name like an honest man." And earlier when it is seen that a letter is not in the prisoner's handwriting the King says, "He must have imitated somebody else's hand." In these instances only one option of several available seems to be open to the King's understanding. One cause for this may be that our language often misleads us. It may seem clear that if a person is not asleep he must be awake. But he could be unconscious. That one is not unconscious does not imply that one must be conscious. He might be day-dreaming or asleep and dreaming. The opposite of moral need not be immoral. One may be a-moral, ignorant, etc. One can be held captive of the model of either-or. If a term has no unique and clear opposite one cannot determine that an opposite term must apply just because the term does not apply.

One is found guilty or not guilty according to law. But apart from this pronouncement or judgment one need not be in fact guilty. Guilt can admit of degree such that one may be slightly or very guilty.

Some of the jury wrote down the word "unimportant," others wrote down "important." This is not unlike the *Regina v. Finney* case in which the Judge did not properly distinguish between "making a mistake" and "inadvertence." These terms need not mean the same thing anymore than "unimportant" and "important" do. It is one thing to "inadvertently" turn on the hot water (while reaching for the cold and thereby scald a patient), but another to "make a mistake" in the faucets. Whether or not the accused is found guilty can depend on distinctions such as this one. If the distinctions are inaccurate the verdict may be wrong.

The King recites from his book, "Rule Forty-two, *All persons more than a mile high to leave the court.*" This may be an instance of a null class (or empty class) as well as a hint about laws which have no application or are no longer enforced. "No dogs allowed," has no application if you have no dog. There are laws based on beliefs no longer held and laws governing the activities of vehicles and objects which are now obsolete and no longer used. It may be for this reason that the King says, "It's the oldest rule in the book." Nietzsche violently attacked certain Christian rules or principles which he felt are outdated and do not apply.

Alice wakes up and runs off for tea and those who read about her adventures may be awakened to the fact that what appears to be a normal everyday life is rather a curious wonderland.

Bertrand Russell writes, "There is no logical impossibility in the hypothesis that the world sprang into being five minutes ago, exactly as it then was, with a population that 'remembered' a wholly unreal past."[1]

Munsat and others believe that there is no such occurrence as remembering or thing such as a Memory.[2]

Lewis Carroll wrote in *Through the Looking-Glass*, " '. . . one's memory works both ways?' [said by the White Queen]

'I'm sure *mine* only works one way,' Alice remarked. 'I can't remember things before they happen.'

'It's a poor sort of memory that only works backwards,' the Queen remarked.

'What sort of thing do *you* remember best?' Alice ventured to ask.

'Oh, things that happened the week after next,' the Queen replied in a careless tone."

In the first place it would appear that we cannot be certain about the accuracy of our memories. How do we know that we remember correctly if we only have access to the present moment? Secondly if memory is regarded as a mental state or mental occurrence or whatever what access do we have to it? Third, does memory have to do only with a vanished past or does it also imply a present and a future? These are only a few of the questions asked in regard to memory. An attempt will be made to clarify the concept of memory and thereby provide answers to some of these questions.

The main difficulty is that of indicating the types of memory there are and giving adequate explanations of how they work. It is here assumed that little progress can be made by speaking about memory or remembering in general. To remember a face is not necessarily like remembering how to swim, remembering that 2 + 2 = 4, remembering a dream, or remembering a future appointment. A tentative classification of memory into types consists of the following. These types will be qualified and clarified in the course of this chapter.

1. *Factual memory*. Often represented by the expression "I remember *that* p." Here p is a statement which is regarded as being either true or false.

2. *Perceptual memory*. "I remember his face." This type is often associated with remembering images.

---

[1] Bertrand Russell, *The Analysis of Mind,* (London: George Allen & Unwin, 1921) p. 159.
[2] Stanley Munsat, *The Concept of Memory,* (New York: Random House, 1967).

3. *Personal memory.* "I remember my swimming in the channel." One reminisces about one's personal experiences.

4. *Verbal memory.* "I remember his words, 'Think of the different points of view from which one can classify tools or chess-men.' " It is important to determine whether any type of memory can be separated from a verbal report.

5. *Prognostic memory.* The White Queen can supposedly remember things that will happen in the future and this strikes us as being a contradiction. On the other hand we do remember events to take place in the future such as "I remember that I have to be at a meeting tomorrow," and "I remember that tomorrow will be cloudy."

6. *Procedural memory.* "I remember how to swim," and "I remember how to play chess."

7. *Dream memory.* "I remember dreaming that. . . . "

8. *Psychological memory.* "I am remembering."

There is overlap between these types of memory as may be indicated by the statement, "I was remembering (psychological) my pretending to (procedural) utter aloud (perceptual) my (personal) opening words (verbal) of the address to be given next week (prognostic).

Memory may thus be classified according to the sorts of objects remembered. There are also representations of the various ways in which these objects are remembered. These are indicated by terms such as recount, recall, retain, repeat, review, retrospect, recount, recollect, remind, reminisce, momento, memoir, memorize. They suggest (a) the past and (b) doing or thinking something again. Memory may be suggested simply by the use of the past tense as in "Yesterday the mail *came*," or by the use of time words such as past, previous, yesterday, before, and expressions such as "It occurs to me." An account of memory must then explain:

1. whether, and if so how, memory relates to the past, present and future;

2. whether, and if so how, memory is doing or thinking something again;

3. what the relationship is between remembering and memory, and the various expressions or alleged synonyms which imply them.

In order to give such an account it will not be possible to speak of memory in general or even of memory types. Instead specific memory statements and illustrations must be analyzed.

One special distinction should be made between (a) first person singular memory statements, e.g. "I remember him," and (b) second and third person memory statements, e.g. "You remembered going," and "He remembered going." This is important because epistemological evidence for #a need not be the same as that for #b. This distinction may be considered in terms of the types of memory, as follows:

1. Factual memory. (a) I remember that p. (b) He remembers that p. Here if all that is referred to is the truth or falsity of p the distinction between first, and second and third person is epistemologically unnecessary.

2. Perceptual memory. (a) I remember Jim's face. (b) He remembers Jim's face. Here the evidence is different in that an observer (b) does not have the memory of image that the first person has.

3. Personal memory. (a) I remember my experience of swimming. (b) He remembers my experience swimming. By definition this sort of memory can only be had by the person experiencing it (a) not by an observer (b).[3]

4. Verbal memory. (a) I remember Jim's words. (b) He remembers Jim's words. The subject may think he knows the words but find he cannot produce them. Both the subject and observer should reproduce the words to ascertain whether they remember them or not. In any case the observer needs to either hear the words remembered by someone else or that person must assert that he remembers the words. The subject, although he may be wrong, need assert neither. He perhaps must, however, say the words remembered to himself.

5. Prognostic memory. (a) I remember my appointment. (b) He remembers his appointment. An observer knows someone remembers an appointment if he knows that person has an appointment and if that person is seen to be present at the right place at the right time or if that person verbally indicates that he remembers it. But I may know I remember an appointment without saying anything or being at the place designated. I may also remember an appointment but not keep it.

6. Procedural memory. (a) I remember how to swim. (b) He remembers how to swim. In this case the observer's evidence might be his seeing someone swim and his knowing that person swam before. My test for my remembering how to swim is to swim. It may, however, be the case that one may remember how to swim in the sense of giving a description of it yet not be able to swim. This case may be represented by the assertion, "I remember how to but am not able to swim." For the observer to know that someone can remember the description of how to swim it is necessary that that person say he can remember how, to describe it or, better yet, give the correct description.

7. Dream memory. (a) I remember my dream. (b) He remembers his dream. Supposedly only the one who had the dream can know that he had it. There may be epistemological difficulty with even this but in any case the observer can only take the word of the one who reports the dream. There are separate criteria such as inconsistency which may lead the observer to reject the report.

8. Psychological memory. (a) I am remembering. (b) He is remembering. Like personal memory only the remembering person can know he is remembering rather than imagining, that is, if there is such a thing as psychological memory.

---

[3] cf Bergson's theory of memory as personal inner intuition.

The observer, e.g. a psychologist, has tests such as electroencephalogram wave patterns, physiological analyses, etc., which may indicate a specific remembering process. However, we do not assume here that there is such a process, occurrence, or mental state. (Note that mental state seems like brain state but "state" is not the sort of thing that can apply to mind, to "something" immaterial.)

Various specific memory statements will now be presented.

"I remember her face."

This instance seems to suggest that we have before us an image. Some hold that all memory takes place by means of images. This may be regarded as a form of perceptual memory.

Hume wrote that sense impressions become ideas and memory is in vivacity somewhere between a strong sense impression and pure passive idea. Imagination is less steady and vivacious than memory. A memory idea can only occur if it is preceded by the corresponding impression, and that idea occurs in the same order as does the impression. If we fail to remember accurately it is due to an imperfection in our faculty of memory. This faculty has the primary function of preserving the order and position of ideas.[4] Thus, for Hume, to remember is to have an idea, image or copy of an original or corresponding sense impression. It is assumed that we may introspect to notice that memory is less vivacious than is imagination or sense ideas and that there is an image there to be seen. Complications arise when details of this view are considered.

An image is not something we see like we see a face. We have no such dual visual system and usually rather say we *have* images but *see* objects. Just what sort of thing or process an image is is not clear. We think it is like a copy of a real object as a picture is a copy. We may here be captivated by the wrong picture of what an image is. Wittgenstein asks if recognizing is comparing two impressions, like carrying a picture with oneself? and Can we in this way look into the past, as if down a spy-glass?[5] Mind and memory are too often thought of as mirrors. Consider (a) a description of an image of one's face and (b) a description of her face. (a) The image is quite fuzzy. There is a dark area, a reddish line border, etc. (b) She had dark hair, a round face, etc.

The attempt to introspect images and "read them off" or just inspect them is not a clear or easy task to perform and it involves many inconsistencies. It is not evidence for remembering her face to say I have an *image* of it. I may be imagining it rather than remembering it. And that one describes one's image of her face does not mean he describes her face unless he knows that the image, vague as it is, corresponds to the face.

---

[4] David Hume, *A Trestise of Human Nature,* ed. L.A. Selby-Bigge, (Oxford: Oxford University Press, 1960), Book I, Part I, section iii.

[5] Ludwig Wittgenstein, *op. cit.* # 604.

But to know the image corresponds to the face is to already assume memory. Do we have another image or idea which tells us that they correspond? Some have assumed something like this in terms of the familiarity theory according to which some ideas just seem familiar. It is as if we have a familiarity image connecting the present image and the face. But how do we know that a familiarity feeling or familiarity image is of the past? (By some other remembering? This would be circular. Familiarity does not imply pastness.) Neither a familiarity feeling or image come dated. Wittgenstein points out that there is no specific feeling such as "long, long, ago."[6] (If remembering were a feeling of familiarity how would we know this feeling is remembering?) Another objection to the familiarity view is that things are familiar not images. Images are usually too vague to serve as things which can be seen twice. We do not say, "I have seen that image of her face before," or "My image of a woman's face is familiar."

Nor does one image appear more vivacious than another to the degree that vivacity can be the mark distinguishing memory ideas from other ideas. "Do you really remember her face?" is not answered by "The image is just right for it to be a memory image."

What would the source of an idea be? (We will speak here about ideas but much of what is said applies to images as well.) Is the idea of the past direct as some naive realists assert? Or can we only know a present idea which somehow represents the past? Consider the following possibilities:

(There exists the special problem of how a sense impression becomes an image or idea and how an object becomes sensed. Nevertheless the object, sensation, idea (or image) terms will be retained for purposes of argument.)

a. The object, sensation and idea exist simultaneously and correspond to each other. We often think this is what an idea consists in to make it a present idea. It is often asserted that memory ideas or images are those we are now experiencing because we can only experience present ideas. On this view "I remember her face," would be a report of a face which is now present. That is, this view stresses the accuracy of present ideas but fails to account for the pastness involved with memory ideas.

b. On the other hand we think there is a lapse of time between the object, sensation and idea. (How we can observe that lapse is another question.) Is there on this view really a strictly present idea of a present object? If we admit that the object precedes the sensation and both precede the idea, even though they all correspond, then what is called present perception already involves the past. The problem becomes that of how we can have access to the present. On this view "I remember her face," involves an idea of her face which was sensed earlier and a sensation of her face which appeared later than the face seen. Thus the so-called present perception of her face already involves the past.

---

[6]Wittgenstein, *op. cit.,* p. 231.

c. A further complication is that the object, sensation and idea may not correspond to one another whether they are simultaneous or consecutive. Thus it may not be possible that one could ever correctly remember someone's face. In this case it may be more accurate to say "I have an image of her face."

d. We may say only my present idea of her face is presently experienced. Is this idea then (a) numerically the same as, (b) the same as but numerically different than, or (c) unlike the previous idea had while seeing her face? "I remember her face," might involve seeing the very same image (perhaps for the first time) of her face as seen earlier, the repeated image of her face, or an image which is not the same as seeing or having a previous image of her face. We do not know that any of these alternatives is possible nor does it seem that we can know if all we have access to is a present idea. We must know by a means independent of the image that the image is of a certain person's face.

It is obvious that when we speak of remembering an appointment, etc., we are not speaking about an image which we have. Psychologists and sense-date theorists inquire into images but when they do they are trying to determine what the evidence might be for their existence. When we say "I remember my appointment," or "I remember her face," we are not in everyday affairs referring to an image which we have. We sometimes do think we have all sorts of clear images but upon looking for them we find they cannot be made out with any sort of detail sufficient to represent, for instance, someone's face. This is not to say that we cannot draw the face or that we cannot describe it more or less accurately or that we cannot recognize the person when we see her. An image is not what we usually mean by remembering nor is it necessarily a clear, directly observable or introspectable object. It is not evidence for remembering one's face to have an image of it. I must be able to describe not the image but the face.

One characteristic of images and vivacity is that they do not have the notion of pastness about them. We think the less clear a thing is the more remote it is. This need not apply in regard to images. Suppose a memory image can be evoked. What age is it? When did you first have it? If it is less clear does it stand for or represent a less recent event than if it is more clear? Images do not in themselves contain the notion of pastness nor can they in themselves guarantee the correctness of memory.

In mentioning pastness it is not here assumed that it can exist as an entity in itself. We observe change not the passage of time or pastness. We observe that one thing is perceived and then is in one way or another removed from our view. This may be our experience of pastness. Thus in speaking of pastness we may instead mean an experience of change or an order of events in relation to each other. Hume may have recognized this when he stated that the primary function of memory is to preserve the order and position of ideas. Memory may be the knowledge that one event changed into another in a certain way. We do not remember seeing her face last week because it feels like it was last week when we saw her. We remember because that was the day we did certain things which cluster around or changed our experience in leading up to seeing her. The event remembered is associated with other events and changes including changes on which time is based. If the notion of time is eliminated as being separate from change we have less difficulty in determining how one may remember the past as such. One need only be aware of various changes which are associated and ordered in a certain way. To say "I remember her face," is to say I know the pattern of its qualities in relation to changes surrounding her face.

In addition, when saying "I remember her face" rather than, for example, "I recognize her face," the object or a picture of the object remembered need not be before us. The relation of events and objects are different when an object is said to be before us than when it is not. It is these relationships that determine whether an event is remembered or not. On this view memory is not reaching back in time itself into something called a past. It is merely noticing an order or pattern of events or objects. When we say "I remember her face," in one usage we know that her face is not present; we do not observe it. The changing patterns and events around one are different than they are when we are dreaming, imagining, visualizing, thinking of, etc., her face.

Just as the test of having a dream is a present description of the dream[7] so the test of having a memory is a present memory report. That one reports a dream or memory does not mean such things reported, once took place. It does mean that the report has a certain coherence about it holding or not holding in regard to other statements we make. Someone may be lying about what he remembers or dreamt. We may find that what was dreamt in fact happened, there really was a lion in the room last night.

This sketch of memory partially accounts for two assertions about the nature of memory, namely, (a) that memory involves a continuity of events (where continuity does not imply time) and (b) that memory involves a type of coherence of knowledge claims. To say "I remember her face," involves our being able to make this statement, to distinguish between this statement and "I imagine her face," to be able to give other statements in support of "I remember her face." If we remember someone's face we must be able to draw it, to describe it (not the image of it), to not act sincerely as if the face is not present, etc.

Some philosophers appropriate memory entirely to the concept of knowledge. We speak of memory claims and memory beliefs. This topic will be discussed when an account of factual memory is considered. To say "I remember her face," is to make some sort of knowledge claim and that claim involves description. Description involves verbal memory just as being able to speak involves knowing (remembering) what the words used mean. In this sense

---

[7] cf Norman Malcolm, *Dreaming*, (New York: Humanities Press, 1959.)

perceptual memory involves verbal memory. We can normally ask for further elucidation and description of "I remember her face," but not of "I remember an image of her face." (We say "I remember her face," rather than literally "I remember seeing her face." We do not ask what the seeing felt like, we ask what her face looked like.) To remember a face is not to somehow repeat it. If the face were repeated it would not be memory. A description is needed in the case of a first and especially in the case of a third person report of memory of a face. Wittgenstein even asserts, "The words with which I express my memory are my memory-reaction."[8]

Returning for a moment to the object-sensation-idea scheme we may find that the scheme is misleading, in addition to the other reasons given, in that sensations may be partially determined by our thought categories, the sorts of knowledge claims we make, what we say to ourselves that we are looking for. An educated musician, an Indian tracker, a detective all sense certain events differently than one another. The verbal description one thinks in or uses may to some extent determine how as well as the sorts of things one senses. Another way of saying this is that it is not clear that sensation can be isolated from intellect, from knowing and describing.

The statement "I remember her face," contains much more than a reference to a face. It is not a reference to an image. It is not a statement synonymous with "face" or "her face." It states a claim about a face which characterizes one person in a context of events and knowledge claims which go to constitute what we call remembering. In speaking of "her face" we want to say we remember the object itself, without using words to represent her face. It is as if we had a wordless thought which is then remembered. Wittgenstein points out that it does not make sense to say one can remember a wordless thought. Memory has no meaning without language.[9] We want to say that we somehow have the whole object when we remember it, as if we could claim "I remember (-」-)." Here the picture is meant to be the actual object but it may also be an image. In neither case is this odd proposition acceptable.

"Her" cannot be represented by an image nor, in spite of mechanistic and physiological attempts, can "remember." These terms as well as "face" function as verbal statements, verbal knowledge or as we will see, as verbal memory.

We think again that an image is some kind of picture we have, that it is on a continuum with seeing, as was mentioned earlier, and that there is a gap between what is not remembered and what once existed which must be filled in by the causal mechanism of a nerve trace or stored image. But if an image is not like what was seen it would make no sense to say something is missing. To say there

---

[8]Wittgenstein, *op. cit.,* #343.

[9]Wittgenstein, *op. cit.,* #343.

is a gap does not mean there is one, if we do not know what sort of thing could be missing. We may say over there is previous knowledge and over here is present knowledge, now what connects the two? We may be misled here into looking for the wrong sort of thing, and looking at the wrong sort of picture.

We sometimes think we have a memory image of something even if we have never seen that thing. One reason we may think this is that we construct a verbal picture of that thing on the basis of what we have read or heard said. One may say he has a clear picture or image of an event that happened in the Civil War even though he was not present. He may have read a description and constructed for himself an image. (On our view an image is not simply a picture however.) Thus if there is any truth in this account the image seen is dependent upon the verbal account.

One interpretation of a memory image that is in keeping with the notion that a memory report is a claim of having knowledge, is that it is a disposition to produce evidence, to describe, draw a picture or perform some other sort of memory evidencing action. This view may be discussed more appropriately, in the next example.

"I remember how to swim."

No images are necessary or need be involved in this sort of memory. It is a statement or claim to knowledge. There may be an ambiguity here between (a) asserting that one knows and can describe or explain the procedure or operations involved in swimming, (b) asserting that one can swim, and (c) knowing how to swim and having known before also.

In sense (a) we sometimes use "I know how to x" interchangeably with "I remember how to x." If there is a past in any clear sense, as we usually think there is, all knowing involves having found out or learned. "I remember" then adds nothing to "I know." In remembering how, there is no fixed object before us but rather a procedure of some sort which requires description. We may claim to remember how to swim in sense (a) because we know we swam. But although we did swim and can still swim we may not be able to describe the process. In this case it may be said that we can swim but do not know *how* to swim. Also it may be the case that one can describe swimming without being able to swim.

Nevertheless if in sense (a) we can describe the procedures involved in swimming we may regard remembering how to swim as being able to make certain correct statements or illustrations concerning swimming. An ability is being attested to and we may find that when we attempt to actually describe the procedure of swimming we cannot. Our basis for thinking we could may have only been based on the fact that we swam—an insufficient basis. In sense (a) to say "I remember how to swim," is to say "I remember how to describe swimming." This is a knowledge claim of an ability. This ability must be distinguished from a disposition for several reasons. (a) A disposition is often regarded as a law-like statement of one's repeated or habitual activity. To remember how to describe swimming need involve no previous statement about swimming. (b) A disposition is sometimes thought of as a tendency to do something. No tendency is involved in asserting "I remember how to swim." The assertion does imply that one could give a description, that is, that one is able to say such and such about the procedure of swimming—not that one has a tendency to give that description. (c) It may be said that it is a disposition to say "I remember how to swim," that under certain circumstances one utters that statement. This view gains support if it is interpreted in terms of Wittgenstein's notion of a language-game,[10] that is, that we learn to use certain words in a linguistic and a situational context. What the words then mean is their use. The statement by Wittgenstein, quoted earlier, is relevant: "The words with which I express my memory are my memory-reaction." (#343)

To say one has a disposition in the sense that one has often in the past performed a certain activity under certain circumstances implies the past. To say that a memory statement is a disposition statement already assumes what is under investigation, namely, whether there is a past and if so how we can know it. The same circular difficulty applies to a language-game which was supposedly learned in the past. However, since on the language-game view the meanings of "past" and "learned" are themselves their use, the past need not be implied. The memory as a language-game view may also retain consistency to the extent that what I mean by memory is the way I now use memory terms. To the extent that a language-game does not imply a past existing somehow it is not circular to treat meaning of memory terms as their uses in language-games.

b, the second sense of "I remember how to swim, is the claim that one can swim. In this case the cash value or meaning of the statement is determined only by whether one can swim or not. If one tries to swim and founders, his statement is false. If he swims correctly, his statement is true. The statements made above in regard to ability and disposition apply here also. Swimming, playing chess, dancing are abilities one has, not images or past events one remembers. To know *how* to do such and such is not necessarily to know *that* such and such is the case. In knowing how, there is no one thing pictured or known but rather a number of things. One may enumerate, as in a book on chess or swimming, all of the activities involved in performing a task. Memory of this sort is different from that of remembering a face. Remembering how is much like a knowledge claim not in the sense that to know is to say or describe a procedure but in the sense that to know is *to do* something. In this sort of knowing the past need not be involved, however. For the memory claim to be true the future, the actual doing, e.g. swimming, is necessary.

c, the third sense of "I remember how to swim," is knowing how to swim in sense (a) or (b) and having known before. This sense depends more on the

---

[10]Wittgenstein, *op. cit.,* #23.

notion of pastness than do the previous two senses. Remembering is partially regarded as knowing before or having known. But although one may remember swimming or that one swam it is quite another thing to remember how to swim. How to swim is not a thing to remember but rules or procedures or, in sense (b), a claim regarding ability or future action. When we remember how to do something it is not necessary to remember the circumstances in which it was learned. One may remember the circumstances but still have forgotten how to swim. One may remember being taught calculus in a certain classroom but not remember how to do calculus.

Still one has the knowledge *that* he did know how to calculate before. This is not the knowledge *that* he calculated but the knowledge that he knew how to calculate. But knowing that one knew how to calculate does not mean one now knows how to calculate. We think that when we say "I remember how to swim," we have two things and a causal relation between them, a past knowing how causing a present knowing how. A past knowing how is not the sort of thing that can function as a cause. A present knowing how is not merely a repeated past knowing how or a copy of a knowing how. An ability cannot be repeated, it is not a repeatable sort of thing.

To say I now know what I knew before contains in it what is in question insofar as the past tense, knew, contains the past. To say "I remember the past," is redundant on the common meaning of remember, although qualifications to such a view are being made here. (Shakespeare's *"remembrance of things past"*[11] is a redundancy.) We do not say "I remember the present," or "I remember the future." Again this is not to say that a philosophical analysis might not give truth to such statements. It is the past and knowledge of the past which comprises part of the problem of the clarification of the concept of memory. To say "I knew," is like saying "I remember knowing." It is not an explanation of "I remember how to swim," to say "I know how to swim and I *knew* how to swim." The question then merely becomes How is it that you knew that and how does one know that he knew? We want to say our having known caused us to now know, as an explanation of memory but it is our having known that is in question. One explanation which may be given for the use of the past tense, other than the notion that time is change, and that its meaning is its use in a language-game, is that memory and past tense statements are certificatory.[12] This view will be discussed in the next illustration.

"I remember it well."

One view of memory may be represented by this paradigm case. We utter this statement when the evidence for it is of a certain type and is not as certain as

---

[11] Sonnet #30.

[12] cf. B. Benjamin, "Remembering," *Essays in Philosophical Psychology*, ed. D. Gustafson, (New York: Doubleday, 1964), pp. 171-194.

knowledge of a present event. That is, we say, "I remember it," rather than "I know it," because we are not sure of it. For one to say "I remember it," is to make a qualification in regard to one's knowledge of it. It means that one cannot now have immediate access to it, and various sorts of statements and inferences are needed to support it. In short, it means that one is not sure of it. In place of "I *remember* such and such," we often say, "I *think* such and such happened." "Think" is also used here as a certificatory term. The evidence for such statements is intersubjective insomuch as the evidence supporting them is intersubjective. One may assert "I remember little Hans," only to discover documents which show that you could never have met him or seen his picture. But it is partially because of the possible appearance of such evidence that "I remember little Hans," is asserted rather than "I know little Hans." Because we think memory is fallable we readily admit having a poor memory or being mistaken about the past. If memory statements are certificatory then what is really meant by memory statements is not that memory is a private process or that we are thinking somehow back to something remote but rather that some statements are more true than others. ("I remember it well," suggests that I may be mistaken about it although less mistaken than "I remember it," and more mistaken than "I know it." Memory so considered depends upon verbal considerations.) This view may be expanded by consideration of the following instance.

"I remember that p," where p is a statement.

We do not say "I remember that her face," but rather, "I remember her face." What characterizes a *that* statement is its stress on *what* is remembered rather than on a so-called process of remembering. Whereas p may be true or false in "I remember that p," her face or an image of it is not true or false in "I remember her face." In "I remember that p," "that" suggests "it is true that," yielding "I remember that it is true that p." *That* statements are often used as paradigm memory statements because they put the issue in the realm of the truth and falsity of objective statements. To see if we remember or not it is thought to be sufficient to determine the truth or falsity of the statement uttered. Memory is regarded as an assertion about truth and falsity. We may then revise "I remember that p," to "It is true that p."

This formula seems to work especially well for statements such as "I remember that 2 + 2 = 4." In this case we do not think we can be mistaken as in some of the certificatory instances given previously. One may say "Well, you merely *remember* that 2 + 2 = 4. That will not do. Tell me when you know that 2 + 2 = 4." But on the analysis given here, remember is appropriated to knowing. It is partially for this reason called factual memory. "I remember that p," may then be rendered as "I know p is true." We regard it as odd to say "I remember that 2 + 2 = 4" is true, because 2 + 2 = 4 is, in one mathematical system, always true. It is an eternal truth which has nothing to do with present, past, future or with remembering. It is an impersonal, intersubjective fact which does not depend upon how it was learned. We may say it was memorized rather than figured out. One may have figured it out but forgotten that 2 + 2 = 4 or that 6 × 9 = 54.

When a fact is so familiar that there is no question about it, e.g. 2 + 2 = 4, we find it odd to say we remember it instead of saying we know it. It is like saying in normal circumstances "I remember that the sun shines," or "I remember that people breathe." It is partially this fact that leads us to appropriate memory to knowledge. By saying that a fact is familiar, reference to the previously mentioned familiarity theory is not implied. Rather a fact here is a statement which is true or false. It is the truth of the statement that is stressed not its familiarity.

Factual memory since it rests on the truth of statements, depends upon language (including the language of mathematics). We do not remember a fact *per se*, we remember, for instance, that " 2 + 2 = 4." (Remembering a fact isn't like remembering a face. Facts are relations of things or ideas as expressed in statements or assertions.) We do not remember truth or falsity *per se*, but rather that two plus two does or does not equal four. Only statements, not things, can be true or false. Factual memory depends on verbal statement. To say "p is a fact" is to say "p is true," where p is a statement. We do not say of a perception that it is true or false.

"I remember that Hartford is the capitol of Connecticut." This assertion is regarded as being true. One could instead say "I know that Hartford is the capitol of Connecticut," (or "Hartford is the capitol of Connecticut,") unless for some reason the certificatory value of "remember" is needed.

In "I remember that she had/has green eyes," or "I remember that the color is/was blue," it is not a perception that is being remembered but it is a statement about a perceived object that is being remembered. These are not statements like "I remember her green eyes." This topic will be treated more fully when verbal memory is discussed.

Norman Malcolm gives as a full definition of factual memory: "A person, B, remembers that p from a time, t, if and only if B knows that p, and B knew that p at t, and if B had not known at t that p he would not now know that p."[13]

Objections to this definition may be given as follows:

(a) On the assumption that knowing involves truth or falsity it may be seen that not every statement we assert as remembering need be wholly true or wholly false. The events described need not be wholly known. The certificatory notion that memory is a partial disclaimer of truth supports the view that knowledge may not be reduced solely to truth or falsity statements.

---

[13] Norman Malcolm, *Knowledge and Certainty*, (Englewood Cliffs: Prentice-Hall, 1963) p. 236.

It would be procrustean and too narrow to require every statement to be true or false. This is especially the case in view of the difficulty we have in ascertaining what truth and falsity are. Many analyses of truth and falsity are available. It does not make sense merely to assert of a sentence that it is true or that it is absolutely true, without a specific context and an agreement about what is to be taken as truth. "P is true," is in itself meaningless or open as to its meaning. We want to know more (or something at all) about a thing than that it is true.

b. The definition of memory need not be accurate for all substitution instances of p. "I remember that $2 + 2 = 4$," is not the same type of sentence as "I remember that it rained." One can remember "$2 + 2 = 4$" from a time, t, but not "it rained" from a time, t. "It rained" does not refer to a fact true now but "$2 + 2 = 4$" does. We cannot assert as the formula requires that "B knew that 'it rained' at t."

c. The formula is circular regarding its assumption of the past if whether the past is involved in memory is in question. To say B remembers p *from a time, t* and B *knew that p at t* assume the past. It already assumes memory.

d. If remembering is regarded as knowing an analysis of knowing needs to be given. Is knowing being able to make further statements, to have an image, to be able to say a statement is true or false, sensing, etc.?

Some of the issues raised in regard to truth, knowing and memory will be further clarified in the following discussion of an instance of verbal memory.

"I remember x," where x is a word or sentence.

We may refer to this as verbal memory. There are several ways in which language enters into the memory picture. (a) We may remember words and sentences, (b) We may remember by means of words and sentences.

In "I remember the poem," there is an ambiguity between (a) saying there is a poem without necessarily remembering the words of the poem or being able to say anything about it. This is like remembering *that*; (b) saying that one is able to actually recite the poem; and (c) asserting that one is able to describe the poem or say something about it without necessarily remembering all or any of the words of the poem. Lewis Carroll wrote in *Alice's Adventures in Wonderland* about Alice's attempt to recite a poem:

"That is not said right," said the Caterpillar.

"Not *quite* right, I'm afraid," said Alice timidly: "some of the words have got altered."

"It is wrong from beginning to end," said the Caterpillar.

Alice still may have been able to describe the poem, tell what it was about or whether it is long or short, etc.

Sense (a) of remembering *that* there was a poem has been discussed. In sense (b) one asserts that he is able to actually recite a poem. Whether he in fact can recite it depends upon his actually doing it. To remember

> "When the blackbird flew out of sight,
> It marked the edge
> Of one of many circles."

it does not suffice as evidence for the first person or an observer to say he can, to say he has the idea and can also put it into words. It is not as if we have the whole thought in remembering it and then put it into words. We do not just see the words in our mind and then say them, read them off. If we have not learned language and do not remember the words we do not remember the poem. It does not help to remember a blackbird flying or a number of circles. Wittgenstein said much the same thing in the following quotations from the *Investigations*.

#649 " 'So if a man has not learned a language, is he unable to have certain memories?' [Someone may say.] Of course—he cannot have verbal memories, verbal wishes or fears, and so on. And memories etc., in language, are not mere threadbare representations of the *real* experiences; for is what is linguistic not an experience?"

#342 "William James, in order to show that thought is possible without speech, quotes the recollection of a deaf-mute, Mr. Ballard, who wrote that in his early youth, even before he could speak, he had had thoughts about God and the world.—What can he have meant?—Ballard writes: 'It was during those delightful rides, some two or three years before my initiation into the rudiments of written language, that I began to ask myself the question: how came the world into being?'—Are you sure—one would like to ask—that this is the correct translation of your wordless thought into words?"

There is then some reason to think that thought is not possible without speech. What would a wordless thought be like? To remember a poem in sense (b) is not to remember an experience but to state the words aloud or to oneself. Also to say "I have a poem in mind. I know I can write it," is not to know or have the poem at all. One must write it to know it. It often happens that one only thinks he can remember a poem and thinks he can write one. When he tries to write or remember it he fails. He may only know what he is going to say when he says it. Saying need not be simply tying up words to somehow already existing thought. Remembering words then is not necessarily having special thoughts but stating that one can utter them, the test for the truth of this statement being to actually utter them. Rather than "I remember the poem," it would be more accurate and complete to say, "I remember the lines:

> 'When the blackbird flew out of sight,
> It marked the edge
> Of one of many circles.' "

Sense (b) may be divided into (1) saying one is able to recite the poem, and (2) stating the exact words remembered.

"I remember the poem," may have the meaning of sense (c) according to which one claims to be able to describe the poem. The description is not an image or thought but is a verbal description. It involves saying something about language. But even if it were a description of an object it would still require a verbal description. In every case of memory verbal skill is required. We would like to say, "This must be wrong. I am directly acquainted with my thoughts and memories. I have them as I have pains." But we say "I sense a pain," not "I sense a thought," and not "I sense a memory." The case of thoughts and memories need not be similar to the case of a pain. This is especially true if we are to specify what we have so called "direct acquaintance" with. It has been often pointed out the notion "direct awareness" has no explanatory force.[14] Without language no specification of thought can be given. To "have a thought" is not to have anything specifically, not an image nor a sensation. What the thought or memory is is what is expressed—or, said differently, there is no such thing as thought or memory as such. Wittgenstein's earlier quoted statement, "The words with which I express my memory are my memory-reaction," (#343) is relevant again here. The number of types of memory we say there are is determined by the number of expressions for and regarding memory that there are. That is, it is determined by the number of language-games we play. Some of these games have been certificatory, prognostic, psychological, verbal, etc. All involve verbal memory in one sense or another. There are many situations from which so-called "memory" terms and their substitutes derive their meaning but no one thing which "memory" names. Memory is not like a string around one's finger without which he could never remember. According to Wittgenstein's *Investigations*, "What we deny is that the picture of the inner process gives us the correct idea of the use of the word 'to remember.' We say that this picture with its ramifications stands in the way of our seeing the use of the word as it is." (#305)

"I am remembering."

This instance appears to imply that remembering is a psychological process of some sort, an act, mental state, neural state, etc. Perhaps this is the picture most people have of memory. We havy seen, however, that when we use memory terms it is not these psychological experiences or psychologist's entities that are primarily referred to. Memory terms form a family of loosely related uses most of which have nothing to do with so-called internal states. We know very little about such states. This is not to deny that something is going on in us when we remember. The point is that what is going on, if anything, is ineffable. It is not clear what is going on in us when we remember, or engage in any other so-called mental process. In saying we do not here deny that there are mental processes or entities it is not at all clear what we are not denying. Because we have words for psychological states e.g. idea, thought, will, intention, concept, memory, etc., does not mean that such states, processes, acts, or faculties (even faculty of forgetting) exist. Words have uses other than that of naming objects. We need not be captivated by the picture of words as names. Memory, for instance, is said to name a storehouse. As has been indicated in all instances so far presented, if

---

[14]Sidney Shoemaker, "Memory," *Encyclopedia of Philosophy*, (Macmillan, 1967).

we do not remember in or with words it is not clear that there can be memory or remembering at all. Having feelings and images, if they could be had and spoken of independent of language would not give us an explanation of how one knows *that* and *what* he remembers. The psychological cause of a memory belief, if there were such a cause, need not be the ground of the belief. The psychological need not be confused with the logical. When a witness is asked to report a past event that report must be consistent with other reports, not with his feelings or images. Except in a psychologist's experiment to say, "I am remembering," is not to be reporting an internal occurrence which is at all clear to us. What is clear is that we do *say* we remember and *say* what it is that we remember.

"I remember that last night I dreamt that. . . . "

This statement may function like "I know that. . . " followed by a story one tells about something he has never really seen. One does not "see_d" things in a dream like one sees real things. And similarly one does not "see_m" things in memory as one sees real things. The subscripts d and m are meant to indicate that seeing_d in a dream need not be like seeing_m in memory. "I dreamt that. . . " is an "I know," sort of statement especially in the sense that what is being reported is a present event, viz., a thought. It may be the case that we do not dream at all but merely have an experience of an incident when we wake up which we can report and which is not like the experience of seeing an actual event take place. We have no test that we had a dream last night except a present experience of some sort. No one else can determine whether one dreamt or not, not even by means of the psychologists rapid eye movement test. This test depends on and so assumes the subject's report of a dream and it is the very existence of a dream which is in question. This account of memory may for the most part be found in Norman Malcolm's book, *Dreaming*, cited earlier. What is of main interest here is that one's knowledge of a dream depends solely on memory. This memory differs from other types in that real events are not recalled but only dream events and furthermore we cannot be certain that dream events ever did take place in the past. Remembering a dream may be knowing a present event or having a present experience only in which we learned to use dream and memory words in a certain way. In this case there would be no remembering at all and it would be inaccurate to use the past tense, dreamt. The dream and memory are dependent on their report. (This does not mean that the report names or represents a thing. It may be a way we learned to use words in certain circumstances, a language-game.) Language is needed for us to offer something as a dream and as a memory. Without it, even to the subject, nothing is clear. We know that dream and memory reports are at least language-games.

"Nothing is less 'intelligible'. . . than the connection between an act of will and its fulfillment."

Bertrand Russell

"What kind of super-strong connexion exists between the act of intending and the thing intended?"

Ludwig Wittgenstein

An attempt will be made to characterize the notion of intention, to show how it is used and give an analysis of why we say the sorts of things about it that we do say.

A. It will be seen that our view of intention depends on our theory of definition, our theory of the meaning of words. What terms, for instance, may we allow to be synonymous with it and what are we to allow as a criterion of synonymity? May we substitute for intention any or all of the following notions such that intention is regarded as a: reason, motive, prediction, desire, want, decision, trying, disposition, mental event, explanation, statement of purpose, foreseeing, or inclination?

B. It will also be seen that our view of intention depends on our view of causality. Does an intention cause an action and if so how does it do it? Various analyses of this question have been given which are dependent upon the view of causality one holds.

In attempting to characterize the notion of intention it seems that we do not have access to an intention as such. For instance, we say "I intend to be at the meeting," but here the intention can only be indicated by a description of what is intended, namely, "to be at the meeting." On this view an intention cannot be described independent of the description of the consequence alleged for it. It is not as if there are two things here, an intention and a description of what is intended.[1] T. Daveney calls the link between intentions which are supposedly logically but not causally connected with actions "identical descriptions."[2]

How could one know what an intention is in itself? Introspection would be something like fishing: it is not certain what one will catch. Perhaps whenever one intends something he notices a tickling sensation. Wittgenstein wrote in this regard that if intention were a feeling can you remember that feeling later? Is it a

---

[1] A view held by A.I. Melden in *Free Action,* (New York: Humanities Press, 1961).

[2] T.F. Daveney, "Intentions and Causes," *Analysis,* Vol. 27, no. 1 (October, 1966), pp. 23-28.

feeling like a tickle? If it is, is it one feeling or a group of many feelings? Is it still a feeling if you repeat after someone else, "I intend to go?"[3] He rejects the suggestion that an intention is any sort of feeling.

If one does have a certain sensation frequently why should this sensation be called an intention rather than a desire or tickle? Is it an intention because it is a feeling of the future? But the future is not part of a sensation as such.[4] Furthermore sensations exist in degrees whereas intentions do not. We do not say "I have a strong intention," or a long, quick or slow intention.

The introspective search for an intention already assumes that we know when we are intending and therefore what an intention is. Melden points out that we can only tell from our sensation that it is an intention after we have been able to describe the sensation.[5] Thus definitions of actions in terms of private happenings are circular as they already presuppose the action. For example, we say, "It is a sensation of *moving my arm*," where "moving my arm" serves to describe the sensation. The same circularity may apply in the case of regarding intention as a sensation. This view conflicts with the view that a cause (or intention) must be identifiable independent of its effect (description of what is intended).

The first difficulty, then, in attempting to characterize intention is that it appears to be definable only in terms of what is intended. We ask, "What was your intention?" and the reply is "To attend the meeting." The reply is in terms of the object of the intention not in terms of a mental state. The reply would not normally be "An odd feeling I have."

We may say "I just have intentions. I should know whether I have them or not." If this were true one should be able to say something about these intentions and people who hold this view cannot. Their resort from being unable to adequately describe an intention is to say "I just know what one is." This yields also a new use of the word, "know." Usually to know something is to be able to say something intelligible about it. To say intentions are indescribable, indefinable, or ineffable is to deny the task of characterizing intentions. G.E.M. Anscombe wrote, "Mental causality is itself characterized by being known without observation."[6] This view, if true, would give us a new type of knowledge but it is evidently a type that we cannot characterize rationally or say anything about. The validity of Bertrand Russell's distinction between knowledge by description and knowledge by acquaintance need not be discussed here.

---

[3]Ludwig Wittgenstein, *op. cit.*, paragraphs #645, #646, #588, #592.

[4]G.E.M. Anscombe suggests also that if intention is just a mental state it would not be concerned with the future. *Intention*, (Oxford: Blackwell, 1957).

[5]Melden, *op. cit.*, chapter 4.

[6]Anscombe, *op. cit.*, p. 24. She does not, however, believe that an intention is just a mental state or cause.

The issue is simply that it is not clear that we do know what an intention is and there certainly is not general agreement about how the concept is to be analyzed. If one does say something about the intentions he has, he finds that there are such difficulties of characterization as are presented here.

It may be noted that the attempt to characterize by means of a definition, although it is not arbitrary and not stipulative, is still an attempt at a definition. This fact may be significant in attempting to define "intention" because if there is a circularity about all definitions there would also be a circularity about the definition of intention. We define terms not things. What then is missing from a definition and may make it seem circular is objects. It will be seen that in specifying that the meaning of a term is its use in a real situation, Wittgenstein avoids this shortcoming of the possible inadequacy of definitions.

Definitions are often found to be circular. Several instances may make this clear:

a. Intention is defined in terms of purpose and purpose in terms of intention. This is a circularity of defining in terms of a synonym and it characterizes lexical or dictionary definitions.

b. 1. Hidden circularity. Ewing said that "x is good" means that one ought to have a favorable attitude toward it. But here favorable includes the notion of good thus yielding "x is *good*" means "one ought to have a *good* attitude toward it."

2. Ross said that certain acts are self-evidently good when we have reached a sufficient mental maturity. But here "maturity" contradicts the notion of self-evidence and includes the notion, good.

3. Ross said moral propositions are a part of any universe where there are moral agents. "Moral" is characterized in terms of "moral." The number of possible circular statements made in regard to the notion of intention cannot be anticipated here. Several additional instances will be given in the course of the paper.

We may say intention may be defined by putting it in a class, seeing what class of things it is most like. But this procedure will not work because it assumes that we already know what an intention is. We may say an intention belongs to the class of mental events but we are not sure how we may adequately characterize either an intention or a mental event such that one can be subsumed under the other. We may, of course, put an unknown in a larger class of unknowns their having one characteristic in common, that of being unintelligible.

It has been suggested so far that:

a. an intention does not seem to name one thing, especially a mental state,

b. an intention is specified by and is not known apart from the description of its object,

c. definitions are often and perhaps always, in some way, circular,

d. any attempt to define intention should try to avoid circularity or indicate why circularity cannot be avoided.

In "I intend to be at the meeting," we see that "I intend. . . " is incomplete and does not make sense without the rest of the sentence. No one says merely, "I intend." Intend functions like "will" in "I will be at the meeting." And, strangely enough, we do ask if then we have a Will such that we can will being at the meeting. So also we ask if we have an Intention such that we can intend to do something. It seems to be generally agreed now that there is no mental state or entity called the Will. The suggestion here is that neither is there an Intention which intends.

"I will," may be regarded as a proper reply to a question, for example, to "Who will help me?" We do not reply to this question, "I intend," nor do we say "I will," if not answering a question. The grammar suggests that intend functions more as an auxiliary than as a verb. Something is needed to complete it.

"I intend," differs from "I go" in that the verb "go" suggests movement whereas intention alone suggests no movement at all. No movement is suggested by "I think," either. To try to define intention alone as something going on in itself may not be possible. And to think that cause as it applies to ideas or that which doesn't move, is used in the same way as it applies to movable objects, appears confused. That is, "This idea causes x," need not be like "This ball causes x."

"Intention" seems to stand for something, to be a variable which may be filled in by the object of the intention. No specific intention is indicated until the variable is specified. In "I intend x," we specify that x = "to go" yielding "I intend to go." Intention in itself would seem to have no meaning in itself in this sense. We do say we have intentions. On this analysis this would only mean that we say things like "I, to go," "I, to travel," etc., but it does not mean that there is something, an intention, which exists alone such that it precedes what is described as intended.

Intention considered as an incomplete expression or a variable is explanatory in several ways. First, what the intention is is exactly identical with what is substituted for the variable. An intention to be an intention must be stated in one sense. One does not say "I have an intention but I do not know what it is." And "I intend to go," is not quite the same as "I intend to be there." These two statements do not express the intentions, because they are the intentions. The way an intention is stated determines what the intention is. This will be more fully discussed. It becomes an extremely important matter in law cases in which exact intentions are inquired into.

Secondly, as an intention is a substituted variable the intention does not exist prior to the substitution and so does not cause the substitution. For this reason also one does not say "I have an intention but I do not know what it is." Intention is not prior here. It would make no sense to say my intention caused the description of the object of my intention or that my intention caused the object of my intention. We would not then say my intention caused me to say either "to go" or "I intend to go." "I intend to go," *is* the intention.

The search for an intention is in part the search for a cause. One wants to say that there must be a cause of "I intend to go," such that I do in fact go. The causal search may look like this:

a. What is the cause of one's thinking "I intend to go?"

b. Does thinking "I intend to go," cause one to go? If so, how?

We may now see that it would be circular to say, "His intention caused the idea, "I, to go," if intention can only be defined in terms of "I, to go." That would yield only "The idea, 'I, to go,' caused the idea 'I, to go.' " But besides being circular it is wrong. An idea cannot cause itself, it is itself. Still we want to say, "Future action is caused by prior intentions." What went wrong?

One thing that went wrong is that we take a cause as a mental state. It was seen that an attack on intention as a mental state is not a difficult one to produce. This is because it is not clear that a "mental state" is independent of external criteria. And external criteria show only what is external and so are not criteria for the "internal" at all. The difficulty is that in searching for an internal cause, a mental state or event, we are confronted with the mind-body problem.[7] The problem is not just how a so-called "inner intention" causes or brings about an observable or external event but how mental events can cause anything mental or non-mental.

In the search for causes, then, it is asked "What is the cause of one's thinking 'I intend to go?' " The answer usually given is that it is an intention itself. On this analysis we could not object to the view that everything we say or think is caused by an intention. In this regard Wittgenstein writes, "But didn't I already intend the whole construction of the sentence (for example) at its beginning?"[8] He denies that this is the case. It is not as if we intend everything we do in advance of doing it, as if we read off an intention like we read off a map. We do not intend each word in a sentence before we utter it.

My statement or thought "Tomorrow it will rain," may be said to be caused by my intention to think that statement. We may in our search for causes be forced to ask what caused one to $intend_2$ $intention_1$ and inquire about the $intention_3$ of $intention_2$ etc. Such a procedure may lead to a regress. This sort of counter argument is not needed as it has already been suggested that there is no such thing as an intention as such. Thus intentions cannot cause anything. "Why did you say, 'I intend to go?' " cannot be intelligibly answered by "I had an intention."

---

[7]The point is mentioned also by Stuart Hampshire in *Thought and Action,* (New York: The Viking Press, 1960) chapter 2.

[8]Wittgenstein, *op. cit.,* #337.

We say "I intend to go," and a search for a cause of this statement seems either futile or not necessary. We know we do do things but we are not clear about inner or mental causes. We do things anyway. We make things happen. It is futile in the sense that we do not know the cause of our having any of our ideas. It is not necessary since we utter such statements whether we know the cause or not.

We do see that if one announces his intention then the event announced often follows the announcement of the event. The agent is then said to have brought about or caused the event to take place. The view of causality employed here is that "x causes y" means that "x is often seen to follow y." For x to follow y, conditions must be favorable and one must not change one's mind.

An unfavorable circumstance would be one where one intends to kill a ghost. An American medical student I once met claimed to have had a real battle with a ghost. Perhaps the majority of Americans intend to go to heaven. That one intends to do something does not imply the existence of what is intended— except perhaps for the person who intends it. We may distinguish between (a) intending a present act of one's own, and (b) intending external acts not all of which are in one's control and which include acts of others. We may also, as Alice of *Alice in Wonderland* claims to do, give ourselves good advice but very seldom follow it.

In speaking about intentions as necessary causes we find that in fact we do not always carry out our intentions. Intentions are not regular enough to support the notion of any kind of strict causality. The idea of a future act is not a sufficient or a necessary condition for that act to take place. It would seem rather that our statement "I intend to go" is more like the colloquial, "I aim to go." We often miss or change our target.

We may note briefly here that there are patterns of behavior, laws admitting of relatively few exceptions. These patterns, however, are often of a circular nature. For instance, one looks back over his actions and then says what he intended to do. Before or at the time of the action he may not have known what his goal was. He now *ex post facto* puts bits of behavior together with his present view of the situation, to construct a unified purpose in his past actions. He may conclude, "I must have intended to help him, otherwise I would not have told him the truth."

Another way of saying this is that a reason (or alibi) need not be a cause. John Passmore suggests that an intention is a pattern of activity, a coherence of actions pointing to a purpose or intention in these actions.[9] One may say that all of one's actions add up to one's having intended to steal a revolver. To

---

[9]John Passmore, "Symposium: Intentions," *Proceedings of the Aristotelian Society*, Suppl. Vol. 24, (1955) pp. 131-146. He also presents a Planning and Neo-behavioristic model of intention. He accepts something of each model in his analysis. This seems to be so that it will account for both the first person and observer's use of intention.

determine one's intentions, for instance, a novelist's, we look at his novels not into his mind. From his works we may find a central theme or pattern and then say that it is that which he intended to write.

The notion of a cause may be similarly considered as a cohering pattern of activity out of which we say this event we will regard as a cause, that an effect. Not everything is important or recurrent enough to be a cause nor must everything we do be intended. As was mentioned earlier, we do not intend in advance every detail of, for example, our going to the store. We do not think when we say "I intend to go to the store," "I will put on my shoes, pick up money from the drawer, take my wallet, walk to the door, open it, get in my car, etc., etc."

To say that the event announced often follows the announcement of the event is not like saying a mental state or tension caused one to have it fulfilled. If intention were such a mental tension, the intention to kill someone might be satisfied by having a chocolate sundae. Perhaps in-tension might suggest to some that there is a tension. If cause must be entirely independent of the effect, such might be possible. T. Daveney gives the example that on the view that intention is separate from what is intended I could intend to go to the station but possibly have that intention fulfilled by taking a bath instead. He rejects, therefore, the view that intention is a mental tension.[10] It may be added that one difference between a prior cause and an intention is that the latter already involves the future.

The intention "I intend to go," is a description which may be said to refer to the event "going." "Going" can be done in many ways, directions, speeds. The event "going" is then a vaguely specified event. If one only thinks "I intend to go," then his intention is as vague as its expression here. I do not mean by this expression that I must also intend or think of all of the things involved in or associated with going. One may intend, for instance, to become a nun for religious reasons but not necessarily so that she will not have to marry, although the latter could possibly be the real intention and not the former. I want to say that the intention is the expression or thought. Writers often say "How do I know what I think until I say it?" I don't want to say, "I have an intention but I do not know what it is." I can say what it is.

One's intention in doing a brave deed on the battlefield may have been "to become a hero." He may have had that idea as he performed the deed. He did not merely have an idea and then put it in words. To know he had a specific intention requires that it be expressed. As expressed, it does not represent a hidden, unexpressed ineffable idea. The idea is the expression.

The idea in an intention depends on how a person phrases (or imagines) it. It depends on how he imagines himself and his environment. The way one's

---

[10]T.F. Daveney, *op. cit.*

intention is stated may be said to affect one's intention in the sense that that is what one's intention is. This is only true of first person intentions (such as "I intend x.")

Bruce Aune states that one intentional statement cannot be substituted for another without remainder because, like belief, intention is a mental state and as such is non-extensional. From "Jones intended to assassinate the king," and "The king is the wisest man in Europe," one cannot validly infer "Jones intended to assassinate the wisest man in Europe."[11] Aune goes on to say that an action may be intentional under one description, unintentional under another, for example. "I didn't intend to shoot the wisest man in Europe; I intended to shoot the king, whom I believed to be the dullest man in Europe." The view that intention statements are not extensional adds support to the view that it is important how an intention is stated in determining what an intention is.

A distinction should be made between intentions as uttered by a person (first person intentions) and intentions ascribed to one by an observer (second and third person intentions). The observer sees a man named Henry thrust a knife in Ed's body. How is he to describe the first man's intention? He can say "Henry thrust a knife into Ed's body." That would seem like an objective description of the situation. We may assume that Henry intended to do what he did do. Even if he is temporarily insane or drugged he may still intend to do what he does in his condition at the time. But he may foresee the consequences of his act and still not intend them.[12] One does not get drunk in order to have a hangover. A hunter may not intend to kill another but by hunting an opportunity is provided for a hunting accident to occur. Merely by engaging in war one may enhance the institution of war, in this case a consequence one may not foresee or want. We cannot assume that because we perform an act that we intended to or that we intended the consequences of that act. Wittgenstein once, while watching leaves blowing about in the wind, said about them, "Now, I'll go this way. Now, I'll go that way."[13] That is, our evidence for intentions is before us and we need not think it is inside us. The observer has to reconstruct and guess at intentions.

Henry may think he is thrusting a knife into Harold who looks like Ed, or doing any number of other things. The observer cannot know the correct description of the event and Henry's intentions. That is, the event may be described (a) in terms of what is objectively observed or (b) in terms of intentions and the moral implications of the event. The observer may say:

---

[11] Bruce Aune, "Intention," *Encyclopedia of Philosophy,* Macmillan, (1967).

[12] A. Kenny suggests that we should not ask the accused if he *foresaw* harm to another but rather determine if he intended it. Anthony Kenny, "Intention and Purpose," *Journal of Philosophy,* (October 27, 1966), pp. 642-651.

[13] Reported by Anscombe in *Intentions, op. cit.*

a. Henry thrust a knife into Ed's body.

b. Henry killed Ed.

c. Henry wounded Ed.

d. Henry (a surgeon) operated on Ed.

e. Henry slipped with a knife, killing Ed.

(b) may be phrased "Henry killed Ed, on purpose," or "Henry intended to kill Ed." The first person intention may be called the expression of intention; the observer view may be regarded as the ascription of intention.

One difficulty in defining such an event as indicated in (a) through (e) above, is that it is not clear that there is just one event differently described. If there were, which description would be given primacy over the others? That depends on our way of looking at and our knowledge of the event(s). We may say Henry, a surgeon, operated on Ed. But when it is discovered that Henry is also an incompetent and careless person "operated" may be a term used ironically. The observer of an event may describe the event in terms of a pattern which he imposes on the situation as when one shouts, "Ed has been murdered," without waiting to find out whether in fact he was wounded or killed.

Because the total past, present and future situation are important in determining intentions, we may say that intentions are defeasible. H. Hart says that foresight is defeasible in the sense that it can only be defined in terms of what will in the future undermine it. Thus he believes that foresight as an action of which we primarily ascribe responsibility cannot be analyzed simply in terms of necessary and sufficient conditions.[14] Intentions are from the observer's point of view what a jury or lawyer finds that they are, as evidence for them is reconstructed. To determine the intention of the defendant one needs to know what would defeat the particular statement of intention. For the court an intention cannot be adequately defined by a fixed definition. It gains its meaning by the reconstruction given it by the court or by the observer(s) who seeks to determine the intention.

Because in this sense intention includes the whole history of an event, Melden does not regard it as a cause, as an event which can cause other events to take place.[15] He asserts that to tell what someone is intending we must check (a) circumstances, (b) further avowals or disavowals made, (c) further actions, (d) feelings betrayed, (e) interests exhibited, etc. Thus an intention is not a single occurrence and so cannot be a cause.

It is not clear that even the defendant as the one who supposedly had intentions knows what these intentions are. He also must depend on memory

---

[14] H. Hart, "The Ascription of Responsibility and Rights," in *Logic and Language* (First Series), ed. A. Flew, (Oxford: Blackwell, 1960), pp. 145-166.

[15] Melden, *op. cit.,* chapter 9. Wittgenstein also says an intention is the whole history of an event. *op. cit.,* #644.

and reconstruct the past. He may rationalize the past, or not be able to express what he was thinking. He may, however, at any moment express an intention for the future and it would seem, except for the qualifications made earlier, that in this case and at this moment he cannot be wrong about his intentions. It is this case which seems to give more certainty to first person statements of intention than an observer's reconstruction of an intention. The types of intention here are:

1. first person's present statement of present intention.
2. first person's statement about his past intention.
3. observer's (jury, lawyers, bystander) reconstruction of the intention.

Type (2) and (3) may both be termed defeasible intentions. They are both *ex post facto* reconstructions. This is not to imply that even an accepted reconstruction could be equivalent to (1). The court often appeals to a model of intention which is termed "what a reasonable man would have done." What a reasonable man is is often what is on trial, what has to be decided. Would a reasonable man in circumstances x, do y? If a husband in crazed anger kills his wife's lover engaged in adultery, would a reasonable man if in crazed anger confronted with the same situation, do the same? It is not clear that we can say that a reasonable man never becomes angry. The courts do accept the husband's act as justified in some cases of this sort.

With defeasible actions of this sort new evidence or a reconsideration of old evidence may cause us to change our minds about someone's intention. We may change our minds about the past as well as about the future. This is one characteristic of intention as reconstructed by an observer.

"Reasonable" often means "one who obeys the law." There is a circularity in regard to defining a reasonable man. H. Sidgwick noted that we often say that is good which a reasonable man does, and a reasonable man is one who does that which is good.

What is noticed about intentions then is that in the most certain first person expression of intention, the intention is neither a sufficient nor a necessary happening for the act to occur. In other cases the intention is reconstructed *ex post facto* and involves that we not know what an intention is until an event happens and then we have a reconstructed pattern of behavior accepted by agreement or convention not the intention. It seems wrong, especially in this defeasible reconstructed sense, to say that an intention or idea causes an action. This is partly what Melden means when he says that a motive does not cause an action like gas causes an explosion; Hume's notion that one prior event such as an inner event, is experienced to be followed by another event, does not apply; a motive explains and presupposes an action, it does not cause it. In addition, Melden has in mind that an idea does not cause a particular physical movement to take place but rather a social event takes place. We are more ready to say one physical event caused another than that a physical event caused a social situation. Melden points out that a physical event is not the sort of thing that can be a cause of a social event. Also a so-called "mental event" like intending is not a nuclear event and so cannot be a cause in the Humean sense.[16] It is not clear, however, why even the most diverse sorts of thing *if they could be isolated from each other* cannot be related causally if by cause is meant high correlation. We can ask "How did that social event come about?" In this sense intention may be regarded as an elliptical statement for a pattern of behavior.

For Melden a thought or idea cannot cause an action, thus an intention if it were an idea could not cause an action. This is because he takes doing and acting as epistemologically prior to ideas and ontologically inseparable from them. Thought derives from doing and assumes it. To the extent that thought in itself is a doing we are robbed of saying that the doing called thinking is itself a process separate from the doing. We cannot have an idea as such. It is always tied to action always used, as Wittgenstein claims, in a language-game seldom if ever the name of a private or separate activity. It is not an idea then that causes an action because idea already includes the notion of action.[17]

The notion of intention rests on laws of human behavior. A deductive cause would be a deduction from a law of human behavior. The more we know about people's behavior the better one can guess a particular person's intentions. Reasonable action becomes defined in terms of the norm. The more we know about a particular person the better we are able to guess his intentions and the "policies" according to which he acts. People do behave more or less orderly. Both Anscombe[18] and Melden[19] use the example to the effect that if someone puts green books all over the roof of a house supposedly "for no reason at all" this would be an unacceptable reason because we would not understand such a person. To claim that there is an intention is to claim that agent and action are intelligible.

We note a particular person's habits and environment. In terms of them we may decide that the defendant was determined to act as he did given the environment he was brought up in. But there is no necessity that one must be determined by one's environment—and it is not clear how many factors we are to include as "one's environment." In any case, an intention as reconstructed becomes an elliptical statement of patterns of behavior and depends for its meaning, on the observer's view of patterns of human behavior. We say "No one in his right mind would have harmed him." Philipp Frank even speaks of the notion of cause as being merely a pattern.[20]

---

[16]Melden, *op. cit.*, chapters 9 and 12.

[17]Melden, *op. cit.*, chapter 11. Ryle in *Concept of Mind* holds a similar view.

[18]Anscombe, *op. cit.*, p. 26.

[19]Melden, *op. cit.*, chapter 9.

[20]Philipp Frank, *Modern Science and Its Philosophy*, (New York: *Collier Books*, 1961), chapter 1.

Character is often said to cause us to act in a certain way. "He said that because he is a liar." The character trait of being a "liar" is a term which is elliptical for all the lies which one has told in the past. "All the lies which one has told in the past" does not cause him to tell a lie. Melden asserts that to say one acts from character is not a causal account. Neither do character traits function as hypothetical law-like statements.[21] One may have a habit of lying but a habit itself causes nothing. His character or habit caused him to lie means that because in the past he has lied we think he will do so in the future. We may be wrong. We do not say when he tells the truth that his character caused him to do it. We should not take literally character traits such as foolhardy, courageous, etc., as being causes such as when it is said, "His courage pulled him through." Courage itself is and does nothing. To find correlations between two actions is, of course, always possible. To say a man acts because of courage is to relate his behavior in a certain situation to a host of similar responses in similar situations. It is in terms of such a law-like sort of statement which Ryle uses to analyze behavior. He gives an account of motives in terms of law-like hypothetical statements which he calls dispositions.[22] Disposition, however, is often thought to have some sort of causal efficacy or power and so goes beyond the mere observance of a pattern of activity. It is often used with causal force as if character, habit, dispositions are entities having a metaphysical power.

An intention may be regarded as a pattern of behavior. By pattern is meant an ordering of a chaos of events which disregards hidden and metaphysical forces which supposedly take place. Melden believes that such an ordering provides one with a better understanding of an agent.[23] Anscombe claims that to give a motive is to say something like "See the action in this light."[24] That is, an action is regarded in one of several possible patterns. Wittgenstein says about an intention: "Why do I want to tell him about an intention too, as well as telling him what I did?—Not because I want to tell him something about *myself*, which goes beyond what happened at that time. . . . not, however, on grounds of self-observation, but by way of a response."[25] What we observe then about intention is nothing more than the pattern of behavior we construct and observe, not an internal state which supposedly acts in a causal manner.

We may now expand some lines of argument presented earlier. One observation about intention was the supposed circularity of intention. We have no definition of intention independent of its object. Melden attempts to show that there is no intention as such. It is a description of a total and complex

---

[21] Melden, *op. cit.*

[22] Gilbert Ryle, *Concept of Mind.*

[23] Melden, *op. cit.,* chapter 9.

[24] Anscombe, *op. cit.*

[25] Wittgenstein, *op. cit.,* #659.

situation such that an intention cannot be reduced to a single occurrence or event. Thus an intention is not a cause of an action.

He has another argument to show that intention cannot exist as such. It is based on Wittgenstein's notion that the meaning of a word is its use in a language-game. That is "intention" gains its meaning both from the language and context or doing situation in which it is used. Stuart Hampshire also holds that intending implies the epistemologically prior category of doing, the practical context. Thought for him presupposes and is bound up with action.[26] Intention as an idea *per se* cannot then exist and so cannot cause an event (that which is intended) to take place because an idea separate from the context, doing or "game" in which it is used is meaningless. An intention as an idea cannot cause an event because an intention if it is meaningful in a language-game already includes the event. It is then as circular to say an intention causes an event as it is to say a word causes the context of its use. Psychological terms, as others, are incomplete until an action is specified.

The term "intention" is ambiguous, meaning either (a) an idea, (b) the object of an idea, (c) both (a) and (b), (d) an idea expressed in a physical situation (which may also be called a pattern of activity). (d) is what is meant by a language-game. "Action" is also an ambiguous term and may mean physical movement or include ideas and other relations. "Action" regarded as an expression used in an appropriate physical circumstance may be regarded as a language-game. "Event" sometimes also means a language-game. Hampshire we saw speaks of the unity of a person engaged in thinking or expressing and the practical situation in which this is done.[27] Just to speak of expressing alone is hypothetical. Thus he says, following Wittgenstein, that we rather use words in (unified) language-games. One may at the age of ten take a life-time vow in a religious faith. This sort of intention is often found to be unrealistic because it ignores future particulars and actual situations.

One should always ask, "Would I do such and such *in that situation?*" But still this test would not suffice. We must be in the situation itself to see what we would do. To see what intentions are, then, we need actual language usage in actual concrete situations, that is, in actual language games. Hampshire, as part of his analysis of intention, presents us with the notion that intention (1) is a language-game and (2) is already involved with the object intended because ideas do not exist apart from practical objects and situations.[28] In sense (1) the notion of intention cannot serve as an explanation. This is the sense in which it is a word used in circumstances, in a language-game. It is not a description or name of itself or an event but is a term we learned to use in certain circumstances.

[26] Hampshire, *op. cit.*, chapter 2, pp. 113-117.
[27] *Ibid.*
[28] *Ibid.*

View (2) may be expanded. We may say "Isn't it remarkable that a chair has so many different aspects?" But what we mean by "chair" is all of the aspects of the chair (as well as other usages). Passmore suggests that seeing a complete intention is like seeing all of the aspects of a table at once.[29] Henry Margenau states that every definition is a tautology except the first time it is stated.[30] We learned the aspects of the chair and defined it later. The definition includes our experience of the chair implicitly. We do not say, "Look from this angle. One of the aspects of a chair is missing." If it is missing then it is not a chair. "Chair" is elliptical for all we mean by chair. Similarly an intention is characterized by certain bodily and contextual circumstances to make it an intention. An intention is not one thing causing what is intended. It is a complex event including what is intended.

A difficulty arises with the view that a chair or intention is elliptical for it includes all that is meant by it. This is that the distinction between the analytic and synthetic becomes hard to maintain. Some argue that the synthetic-analytic distinction is not valid or not clearly made out. No further attempt will be made to decide this issue here but it should be mentioned that the issue is relevant. It is not clear what it means to include the predicate of a statement in its subject nor is it clear what it means to include predicates of intention in the subject, intention.

Along these lines we may find it difficult to distinguish between a human action and a physical event. The physical may include notions which include human observations as well as value judgments. A similar question is raised by Chisholm who asks what Anscombe means by saying that an event is "merely physiological."[31] The physical need not be reduced to a nuclear event any more than a human action need be. On the other hand, a human action may be regarded as a nuclear event just as is a physical event. Melden asserts, however, that this is not the case. His argument depends on a narrow definition of "event" as regards the physical and a broad and even circular definition of event as regards human action. For him intention is an explanation rather than an event. An explanation or reason is not the same as a cause. This may be true mainly of one use of intention, namely, where "He does x intentionally," means "He does x *for a reason*," whereas "I intend to go" need not be done for a reason. We sometimes mean by "intentionally" merely that one "meant" to do it or one was aware of doing it, though not necessarily for a reason.

Perhaps a so-called physical cause can be viewed as including its effect as much as can a human action. We have to decide how much we are to include in the cause or stimulus and how much to leave out. If we include too much, we may include the effect.

---

[29] Passmore, *op. cit.*

[30] Henry Margenau, "Meaning and the Scientific Status of Causality."

[31] R. Chisholm, Review of Anscombe's *Intention, Phil. Rev.*, (January, 1959) pp. 110-115.

The notion that x is a necessary or sufficient condition for y stands in the same need of clarity. How much are we to include in the notion of a condition? The notions of cause, event, condition are vague and if too inclusive or if expanded may well become specified in a circular manner. They may be causes of an effect in the sense that they include the very notion of the effect.

A consideration and organization of our notions of cause should give some light to our views of intention. The position we take in regard to causality organizes and determines the views we take of intention and its object.

A. When the cause is not regarded as being separate from the effect:

We may say that the notion of a cause already includes the notion of its effect. Arguments for this view would be as follows:

1. There can be no cause without an effect. If there could be "cause" would be meaningless. "Nothing was caused by x," does not make sense. Cause is something we sometimes refer to only in retrospect, not before the effect has taken place. We do not know the future as future, that a cause will have a certain effect, until the future becomes present or past. If we say we find a cause without an effect we may say it is not a cause. If a cause is a cause, it has an effect by definition. Also if we say we find an effect without a cause it is not an effect.

2. Our description of a cause may be circular in including in it the notion of effect, for example, the cause of one end of a top rising when spun is that that is one of its properties. J. Feinberg calls it an "accordion effect" to define an act in terms of its consequences because the consequences can be expanded or contracted at will.[32] J. Ladd thinks it does make a difference how an act is described because the definition includes different ethical statements that should not be, as he puts it, "whittled away."[33] It does make a difference what is to be included among the act and what among the consequences, for instance, whether an action is to be described as the moving of a hand on a trigger, the killing of a man, the killing of an enemy, the murder of a friend. Ladd calls the "accordion effect" also an ethical effect. An example given of the incorporation of a consequent into an action is seen by the difference between:
   a. He saved her life.
   b. He pulled her out of the water.
   (a) includes, Ladd asserts, an ethical consequent in a way (b) does not.
Intention may be regarded not as an idea but as a description of a situation in retrospect or including both past, and present, and future, that is, the whole history of an act. Also we may say that to tell if x is a cause we must see if it occurs prior to y. If it does it is a cause. This procedure, however, includes the notion of effect in determining the cause.

One of Hume's views of cause is that one event merely follows another. "Follows" here means "comes after in time." Thus it would make no sense to ask if time is involved in the notion of cause since cause is defined in temporal terms. But what is in question is Does one event *come after* another?, Does cause have temporal direction?, Is the object of an intention merely future to an intention? To say that causality regarded as "x follows y" applies is to say that

[32] Joel Feinberg, "Action and Responsibility," *Philosophy in America,* ed. Max Black, (New York: Cornell Univ. Press, 1965.) pp. 134-160.

[33] John Ladd, "Symposium: Ethics and the Concept of Action," *Journal of Philosophy,* (November, 1965), pp. 633-645.

the concept of present or past, and future applies. Therefore we cannot without further examination and without circularity assume that an intention must be a causal notion.

A term way include a cause and effect. "Melting" means that a substance becomes warmer and liquid. It is redundant to say that the melting was caused by the increase in temperature.[34] Furthermore, the warmth and melting can occur simultaneously rather than successively such that to speak of cause is inappropriate.

To say that an intention is "fulfilled" may not mean that the intention occurs first. The term may mislead in suggesting futurity where there may be none.

Henry Margenau and Philipp Frank state that the causal principle itself is a tautology.[35] In "x state causes y state," "state" is undefined. Thus the causality postulate reduces to a definition of what is meant by "state," and this procedure involves a tautology. We just redefine "state" with fictitious properties until the same type of states are always followed by the same type of states. A law is a definition which is a product of human imagination, according to Frank. He says that questions such as those of cause are not questions like "Is that thus or so?" but rather "Can we paint the picture in this or in that style, or in both?"[36]

(3) Cause may be regarded as an explanation or reason. Human actions are not causes in the way physical objects are. An intention does not cause anything, a person does. We refer to a mosquito as the cause of malaria and we refer to a person as the cause of his actions but we are not sure as we are with the mosquito what in the person is the cause. We then often say that we have reasons for human action in the sense that a reason is an explanation of action rather than a naming of a single previous event. Reason is a broader term than cause and can include past, present, and future in its account. We need not think that an event is one thing such that the relation between an intention and the object intended is a one to one relationship.

(4) Can an intention to go to a movie cause one not to go? or to go elsewhere instead. As was pointed out earlier, if an intention is a cause, is independent of the effect (or that which is intended), then my intention to go may even cause me to stay. This seems false and so a closer connection between an intention and what is intended must be looked for. On this view an intention would not be a cause of a *particular* or specific event.

(5) Intention may be regarded as having a meaning in a language-game, in Wittgenstein's sense, and so not be regarded as itself a cause or explanation of anything. It would then be only a word which is *used* in such and such situations.

The analysis of intention in terms of trying[37] puts a stress on the situation and on objects rather than on hidden internal events. The notion of trying,

---

[34] This is what D. Gasking meant when he said that "x melts" means "high temperature causes x to become liquid," in "Causation and Recipes," Mind, LXIV (1955), pp. 479-487.

[35] Henry Margenau, *op. cit;* Philipp Frank, *op. cit.*

[36] Philipp Frank, *op. cit.,* chapter 1.

[37] Hampshire, *op. cit.*

although it tends toward accounting for what a language-game can account for, nevertheless is not the same as intending. One can intend to do something without trying to do it.

One of the reasons why a language-game analysis is interesting is that it includes both descriptions and objects. On other analyses of meaning the relation between objects and language remains a problem. A wedge is driven between them such that we say, "Well, I know what an intention is and I do not need a description of one," or "I can describe an intention, but that yields only a description not the intention itself." The point is that there is no one object or idea as a referent of an intention.

(6) The notion that an intention is a defeasible notion, similar to a reason or description, as determined *ex post facto* by the law courts or interested observers, offers support to the view that the intention is not a cause of the intended event.

Different people look at the same event as having different causes e.g. a religious cause, a statistical cause, etc. We question what is to be regarded as *the* cause of an event and how that event, cause and effect are to be described.

Cause and effect on one view of cause ranges over much of past experience and interpretations because it applies to classes of events not individual events. To say one event causes another invariably, we could not be dealing with two individual events but only two events which are similar in certain respects to each other. If the same event does not repeat itself it cannot function as a cause—and the same individual event cannot repeat itself. This heat cannot cause this water to boil invariably.

But there may be a circularity in attempting to determine which event is relevant to another event in the proper way so as to function as a causal type. If we wish to define cause we do not want to assume the notion by specifying the conditions under which alone cause can work. That is, we do not want to presuppose what it is about events of type A which causes events of type B. We should not define an event too narrowly for an event to recur. But when we broaden the definition we begin including factors which directly or indirectly relate to the effect.

It may be noted here that the notion of meaning as defeasible is close to the pragmatic theory of meaning[38] whereby the meaning of a term is determined by its future consequences. The pragmatic theory of meaning is analogous to the view that the truth of a theory is determined by its results, by whether it is found to be fruitful or not.

B. When the effect is not included in the notion of cause:

The odd thing about an intention causing the intended act is that whereas usually the cause, as past or present, comes before the effect, as future, with

---

[38] As represented by Charles Peirce.

intention the intention, as past or present including the idea of future, comes before the future. The idea of future, however, may well come before the future state of affairs. It is not circular to say "I intend p" is followed by p. "I intend p" is an intention not a state of affairs here. If I say p_1 is followed by p_1 then the situation is circular. That is, it is not contradictory to say a description of a state of affairs is followed by the state of affairs described, as it would be to say the description of the state of affairs$_1$ is followed by the description of the state of affairs.$_1$

If however we mean by "future" not an entity in itself but merely a change of state of affairs what is odd about intention becomes revised. Thus an event becomes a change in a state of affairs. We have then simply two somehow demarcated events related to each other. This does not commit us to assuming time or its passage as such. This view of causality is similar to the functional or correlative view of causality. An example of the function view may be represented by a formula in physics such as $d = rt$. One may equally well say $r = \dfrac{d}{t}$ or $t = \dfrac{d}{r}$. We do not say one factor came before or caused the other. The factors may be simultaneous.

If an auto pulls a trailer which is tightly attached to it, the forward movement of the car is sufficient for the movement of the trailer and the forward movement of the trailer is sufficient for the movement of the car. The movement of either is necessary for the movement of the other. There is no temporal gap here. The events may be regarded as contemporaneous.

On Hume's view of cause as correlation as it is frequently used in science, two events are statistically correlated such that one is often seen to go with the other. A. Kaplan supports the view that causal explanation should be regarded as statistical explanation and this he calls "Non causal explanation."[39] Bertrand Russell says that any case of frequent sequence is a cause, even that night is the cause of day.[40] On the functional view two or more factors are seen to vary with each other. Time need not be a factor here, especially as a factor independent of change. On this view we need not say whether the first event caused the second or the second event caused the first. On this view the state of affairs intended may cause the intention or vice versa.

The law-like nature of correlation and functional causes is very close to the notion of dispositions especially if disposition is not considered as a mental set or as having causal efficacy. Also on this view the intention is allowed to be unmysteriously highly relevant to the event intended, and the event intended is highly relevant to the intention. That is, (a) the fact that I did an act means that

[39] Abraham Kaplan, "Non Causal Explanation," in *Cause and Effect*, ed. Lerner, (New York: The Free Press, 1965) pp. 145-155.

[40] Bertrand Russell, "On the Notion of Cause," *Mysticism and Logic*, (New York: Doubleday, 1957), pp. 174-201.

I probably intended to, and (b) the fact that I intend to do an act means that I probably will do it. To determine what "probably" means here actual statistical or functional relation figures would have to be obtained. But also on this view of cause an intention to go may "cause" one to stay home, assuming as we are that intention and the object of intention are regarded as separate events.

The view that cause is a power or force is ignored here because it seems to lack intelligibility. It also gives time a one direction primacy. If time were merely change it would have to be determined which way change works. It is not clear what this means. The notion of cause as power also is often regarded as being a necessary as well as an inherent connection between a cause and an effect, that is, a cause compels its effect.

It is usually seen that necessity is too strong a notion except in those cases where the effect is included in the cause by definition. Even scientific laws may have exceptions. That is, laws are thought often to be actual uniformities rather than inviolable rules.

The notion that cause is an effort is related to intention by means of the view held by Hampshire and others that intention can be analyzed as trying to do something. As was mentioned earlier, it may be seen that we can intend something without either trying to or trying to bring about the object intended.

A further question is how an intention connects with the alleged object intended if the situation is thought of in terms of temporal contiguity of two events. If two events are in fact separate and endure then that one changes to become the second event would mean that event$_1$ did not cause event$_2$ but rather *became* event.$_2$ Or it would mean that somehow a static event is the cause of another static event? If this is the case it is hard to see how a static event can be an efficacious cause. If the events are static it may not matter whether they are close (contiguous) or not.

If an intention causes an action to be performed, does the intention still remain an intention throughout the process? Is it the intention itself that causes the action or is it rather the person who intends that brings about the action by a manipulative technique? D. Gasking maintains that a cause is like a recipe for manipulating objects so as to bring about a certain change.[41]

Bertrand Russell points out that two distinct events cannot be contiguous in time and still be causally necessary because there is always a lapse of time between cause and effect which can allow something to prevent the expected result. E. Nagel maintains that there are no precise criteria for deciding when events are contiguous.[42] One advantage of the analysis of cause as a functional relationship is that it dispenses with both the notion of before and after (temporality) as well as the notion of intermediates between events.

---

[41] D. Gasking, "Causation and Recipes," *op. cit.*

[42] E. Nagel "Types of Causal Explanation in Science," *Cause and Effect* (ed.) by Lerner, *op. cit.,* pp. 11-32.

Intention considered as prediction would conform to this analysis. Our intentions often are not fulfilled and are separated by a great lapse of time. Cause need not be continuous or contiguous in time especially if the process involved depends on a great number of unknown intermediary factors. Psychologists can often say what will happen to a person's behavior five years from now but not one second or ten minutes from now. He is not aware of all the intervening factors. We may predict an event yet not know the intervening factors and, of course, our prediction may be wrong. The same is true with intentions. A man may intend to do something but he cannot effectively predict that he will do it. He does not know all of the sufficient conditions necessary for the predicted event to occur. We may know some of the things that must occur but not the probabilities with which such changes take place in nature.

It is often said that human behavior is teleological.[43] With a physical organism we may state what a self-regulating system is and so within that system specify the function of a specific organ in respect to the whole system. With human behavior it is not clear what a self-regulating system would be like or what mechanisms are involved such that we may readily say that human behavior is purposive in the sense that man proposes a number of intentions. The best laid plans, however, go astray. It is because one cannot specify all of the possible conditions of an action such that nothing can go wrong that H. Hart regards action concepts as essentially ascriptive and defeasible.

If by teleology is meant that the later event intended causes the intention, it is not clear what this could mean. The issue of even a prior idea causing an action was seen to involve difficulty. It would be harder to understand how a later event produces an earlier one. It would seem that the situation is not teleological at all even if an idea of an event causes a later event. Certainly the later event does not occur before the intention nor does it cause the intention to occur. We may regard the object of intention as existing prior in idea, to the actual fulfillment of the intention. But this is not teleology in the sense that it is opposed to causality. It rather depends on equivocation.

It would seem that one can always find some abstract or general purpose in a pattern of events to be seen as responsible for the existence of that pattern. An observer may regard a pattern as if it tended to or was caused by a final cause.

It is seen that the notion of intention need not be reduced to one notion of cause and effect at least until a clear and specific account can be given for the notion of cause and effect. Henry Margenau states that in fact there is no

---

[43] a) Charles Taylor, *The Explanation of Behavior,* (London: Routledge and Kegan Paul, 1964), chapter 3.

b) R. Chisholm asserts that purposive action is an irreducible notion (Teleology is indefinable.). We must take "A did x *for the purpose of* y" as primitive. "Symposium: Action, Motive, and Desire," by R. Chisholm, Journal of Philosophy, Vol. LXI, No. 20 (Oct. 29, 1964), pp. 613-625.

plausible way of defining cause and effect and that physics knows no such law.[44]

It may be seen also that if we are to speak of human freedom as intention and carrying out our intentions, the issue is not as simple as merely having intentions and carrying them out. The various analyses of intention as are given here need also to be considered.

It has been shown then how intention may best be characterized, why various people have said the things they have about intention, and how the problem of characterizing intention depends on our notion of meaning and our notion of causality.

---

[44] Henry Margenau, *op. cit.*

A comparison will be made here between some of the major tenets of Zen Buddhism and the ordinary-language philosophy of L. Wittgenstein. The attempt will not establish that they are identical, that if we look closely, we will see how nicely a certain form fits itself. What will be seen is that there are significant similarities to be found, and that a knowledge of these contributes to our understanding of each philosophy.

In order to ensure concreteness and accuracy, the comparison will be based on statements only from Wittgenstein, some Zen sayings, Koans, and Haikus. The Koan is a theme or statement or question given the Zen pupil for solution and understanding. It will, hopefully, lead him to Satori or enlightenment. It is not assumed here that all sects of Zen stress Satori, nor that there is one single view which is true of all adherents of Zen.

The Rinzai sect of Zen Buddhism places great stress on the Koan as a way to enlightenment. Rinzai monks are given books of these to read and examine.[1] To this extent language does play a part in some quarters of Zen. No attempt is made to compare ordinary-language philosophy with adherents of Zen who say nothing but sit for years in silence facing a wall. The Haiku, is a very short poem which, in the case of those cited, is an expression of the Zen attitude.[2]

To begin, we see that both Wittgenstein and Zen reject philosophy. Wittgenstein writes,

"Most of the propositions and questions to be found in philosophical works are not false but nonsensical." (*Tractatus,* 4.003);
"For philosophical problems arise when language *goes on a holiday.*" (*Philosophical Investigations,* 38);
"Let us ask ourselves: why do we feel a grammatical joke to be *deep?* (And that is what the depth of philosophy is.)" (PI, 111)[3];
"When we do philosophy, we should like to hypostatize feelings where there are none." (PI, 598);
"When we do philosophy we are like savages, primitive people, who hear the expressions of civilized men, put a false interpretation on them, and then draw the queerest conclusions from it." (PI, 194)

Master Tokusan burns his books and says, "All our understanding of the abstractions of philosophy is like a single hair in the vastness of space." Here

[1] *Mumonkwan* and *Hekigan-roku* are two important collections.
[2] The Koan examples are taken from the writings of D.T. Suzuki on Zen Buddhism and the Haiku examples are mainly from R.H. Blythe, *Haiku* (4 vols.), Japan: Hokuseido Press, 1949.
[3] Ludwig Wittgenstein, *Philosophical Investigations, op. cit.*

adequate wholeness is stressed as well as a disdain for philosophy. Even to say that you are the Buddha, you and the Buddha are one, the Buddha is living in you, are too flat because they are too abstract and conceptual. The stress is on action, not on reason, as we will see. Buddha himself had no use for philosophy.

The attack on philosophy involves the following views by the adherents of Zen and by Wittgenstein.

a. The claim that they are not themselves doing philosophy; that they are showing rather than telling.

b. that therapy replaces philosophy.

c. that theory should be replaced by attending to the concrete and particular.

d. that ordinary language use and everyday situations should be our guide rather than philosophy.

e. that action should be our guide rather than reasoning, description rather than explanation.

f. that fixed philosophical definitions and categories give a partial picture as compared with actual living practice.

Both Zen and Wittgenstein's view will here be referred to as philosophies even though Buddha and Wittgenstein claimed they were not doing philosophy.[4] The above attitudes toward philosophy are part of the overall views of each philosophy. These views may be outlined as follows:

I. Negative Side. Breaking Down Traditional Notions of the Following
   A. Philosophy
   B. Mind
   C. Oppositions
     1. subject—object
     2. self—other
     3. internal—external
     4. private—public
   D. Identity and contradiction
   E. Definition and naming (There is no hidden, fixed, or final way.)
   F. Causation, explanation, reason

II. Positive Side
   A. Stress on nature
     1. the concrete and specific
     2. doing
     3. the everyday and actual
     4. the total concrete situation
     5. description, not explanation; showing, not telling
     6. ordinary language and the colloquial
   B. Humor as insight
   C. Revealing statements. (The model, Koan and Haiku.)

---

[4] Note that Wittgenstein entitled one book *Philosophical Investigations.*

The above characteristics as applied to Zen may appear to leave out the essential point, namely, that to say anything about Zen is to misinterpret it or that about the Zen enlightenment or Satori nothing can be said. Satori is supposedly a private experience to which reason, analysis, and description have no access. It is a mystical, ineffable experience. We think of knowing as being able to say something about something. The question arises as to whether we can know what we supposedly can't say anything about, in this case, Satori. Perhaps then all writings about Zen are nonsense. Zen writers do not deny this as several Koan's will later indicate. Here we speak, however, mainly about the techniques of Zen such as the sayings which help one achieve Satori, not about Satori itself.

Wittgenstein similarly rejects statements which he himself makes, as being higher level philosophical statements. Because he holds that the meaning of a statement is its use in a language-game,[5] he is forced also to maintain that the meaning of his own statements is their use. (Meaning is not for him something separate from or accompanying his statements.) It is not, however, clear why Wittgenstein does not allow the universe of discourse of philosophy to remain as a proper sort of language-game which one can learn like any other. He may *say* he is not doing philosophy and the Zen Buddhist may say he has no philosophical view, but such assertions seem as self-contradictory as the statement "I am not now presenting a statement."

What Wittgenstein does mean, however, is that his meaning shows itself in his language but cannot be about itself and furthermore, that there is no higher level to appeal to. The only appeal is to everyday or ordinary language. Actual use then becomes that about which nothing can be said. It is the given, bed-rock. Perhaps Satori, or the Zen experience is like that also—experience of just what happens, nothing more. But that's just it—what happens we are not allowed *to say*.

Both philosophies are thought of as having therapeutic effect. Both claim to be philosophies which undo philosophy and so lead us back to the concrete actual real world. The Zen Buddhist takes the supreme mark of the integrated (well) man to be the absence of a mind divided by irresolvable and artificial oppositions such as that of subject versus object. Wittgenstein says we often go wrong when we are held captive of a wrong sort of picture (PI, 115) or concept, for example, that the word "mind" just *names* a thing or entity. Do not think that "I describe my state of mind" is like "I describe my room." (PI, 290). The following statements make Wittgenstein's therapy clear:

"The results of philosophy are the uncovering of one or another piece of plain nonsense and of bumps that the understanding has got by running its head up against the limits of language." (PI, 119)

---

[5] A language-game is the use a word has in a certain situation such as saying "Hello" when greeting someone. The language-game here is greeting and the meaning of "Hello" is its use in greeting. "Hello" supposedly has no other hidden or independent meaning here.

The exposing of and correction of such nonsense serves as therapy.

"A philosophical problem has the form: 'I don't know my way about.' " (PI, 123)
"The philosopher is the man who has to cure himself of many sicknesses of the understanding before he can arrive at the notions of the sound human understanding." (RFM, p. 157)[6]
"When philosophers use a word—'knowledge,' 'being,' 'object,' 'I,' 'proposition,' 'name'— and try to grasp the *essence* of the thing, one must always ask oneself: is the word ever actually used in this way in the language-game which is its original home?—What *we* do is to bring words back from their metaphysical to their everyday use." (PI, 116)
"There is not *a* philosophical method, though there are indeed methods, like different therapies." (PI, 133)
"The philosopher's treatment of a question is like the treatment of an illness." (PI, 255)
"A main cause of philosophical disease—a one-sided diet: one nourishes one's thinking with only one kind of example." (PI, 593)

This sort of disease is that which Zen also attempts to cure by a release from certain fixed categories.

"What is your aim in philosophy?—to show the fly the way out of the fly-bottle." (PI, 309)

In Zen, the therapy is achieved in various ways as will be seen. Suzuki tells us that Zen is practical for psychiatry. "It is the object of Zen, therefore, to save us from going crazy or being crippled."[7]

We are told by Wittgenstein and adherents of Zen not to meddle with the natural flow. If we do, we distort and so have need for therapy. The therapy sometimes involves, in Zen, one's answering one's own questions, working one's problem out for oneself. (A Zen saying is, "If you do not get it from yourself, where will you go for it?") This expression of individuality is seen in the vulgar assertion about Buddha, "When you utter the name of Buddha, wash your mouth out." Zen supposedly has the therapeutic effect of returning one to oneself. It is not yet clear, however, what that is like. The therapy for Zen revolves around the ineffable Satori.

But Wittgenstein's therapy of returning to ordinary language, involving as it does the question of what is and what is not ordinary, may involve the ineffable also. This is especially so if we can only answer the question in ordinary language.

(The translation of Koans and Haikus and sayings is often free. The translations that appear here are those found in Suzuki and Blythe in the texts mentioned earlier.)

Monk: "How may I enter the Way?"
Master: (pointing to a mountain stream) "Do you hear the sound of that torrent? There you may enter."

---

[6] Ludwig Wittgenstein, *Remarks on the Foundation of Mathematics,* (Oxford: Blackwell, 1956).

[7] D.T. Suzuki, *Zen Buddhism: Selected Writings of D.T. Suzuki,* ed. William Barrett, (New York: Doubleday, 1956), p. 3.

This Koan stresses the concrete, the everyday, the immediate, the actual, the natural, the identity of oneself with objects. The breaking down of the distinction between oneself and object is indicated by suggesting that one may enter the Way by entering the torrent, by becoming the torrent. For the moment we need not be concerned that Wittgenstein might call this a misuse of grammar.

> Monk: "How may I enter the Way?"
> Master: "Do you smell the mountain laurel?"
> Monk: "Yes."
> Master: "There, I have held nothing back from you."

Here the notion is stressed that the actual is a familiar and everyday sort of thing, perhaps too familiar for we sometimes think that there must be something hidden behind what we see. There is not. Wittgenstein wrote, "The aspects of things that are most important for us are hidden because of their simplicity and familiarity. (One is unable to notice something—because it is always before one's eyes.)" (PI, 129) and "And if I say it is hidden—then how do I know what I have to look for? I am in a muddle." (PI, 153)

(Adherents of Zen do say that their sayings point beyond themselves to the transcendent, but they also say that they are themselves only and should be taken at face value. Relevant to this is the notion of contradiction discussed later.)

Wittgenstein supports these three main ideas, namely, the support of the concrete and actual, dissolving the distinction between, for example, subject and object, and rejection of the idea that there are hidden and theoretical entities. He stresses the actual and concrete by stressing actual language usage as it was originally learned. We will see, too, that both Zen and Wittgenstein stress the colloquial, that is, actual usage.[8] The way Wittgenstein dissolves the distinction between subject and object is not so easy to see. It involves the fact that Wittgenstein asserts that words don't usually name but rather have their function in a particular situation. "What d'ya know?" for instance, is not an inquiry into someone's inner state of knowing but rather functions to entice someone to say something. The error we, supposedly, usually commit is that we think words for inner states usually *name* or *describe* entities, states, or inner processes. He thus asserts that words for feelings, emotions, inner functions, inner powers, notions such as "I," "self," "explain," "true," "certain," "identity," "time" do not name things or have fixed definitions. "Will," "memory," "imagination," "wish" are not names for inner things or processes. A person knows of himself, and the very notion of "himself," by means of an intersubjective language learned in a public situation. This undermines the notion of there being an inner, private mental world as opposed to a public world. This attack on privacy and the

---

[8]In the psychiatric work, *Games People Play*, by Eric Berne, (New York, Grove Press, 1964), colloquial language is stressed and is significant in his therapy.

breaking down of the distinction between subject and object is another place where Zen and ordinary language meet.

It may be pointed out, however, that Zen often stresses the inner, private subjective experience. And Wittgenstein, too, sometimes admits that some inner processes may be taking place—it's just not clear how we can know what they are. Again we are confronted by the ineffable. ("So we have to deny the yet uncomprehended process in the yet unexplored medium. And now it looks as if we had denied mental processes. And naturally we don't want to deny them." (PI, 308) In light of the Zen view that language and its categories cannot fully describe, they assert that even the seeing into oneself which they advocate is too binding and is inaccurate.

Wittgenstein seems to have us imagine a sort of soulless tribe as a way of getting rid of the picture, the 'accompanying' picture, that is, getting rid of the notion of supposedly hidden private states. The theme runs through the entire *Philosophical Investigations*. Man is thought of as being a public, doing, living creature not possessed of a private special world.

"An 'inner process' [if there are any] stands in need of outward criteria." (PI, 580)

The distinction of subject and object like that of private and public is thus undermined.

Kuang cut off his arm to show that he could endure what is necessary in order to learn. At this Bodhi-Dharma said that the doctrine of Buddhism is not to be sought through another. (A statement stressing the subjective and private.) But consider:

Kuang: "My soul is not yet pacified. Pray, master, pacify it."
Bodhi-Dharma: "Bring your soul here, and I will have it pacified."
Kuang: "I have sought it these many years and am still unable to get hold of it."
Bodhi-Dharma: "There! it is pacified once for all."

"There is no place to seek the mind;
It is like the footprints of the birds in the sky."

Monk: "What is the Tao [the Way, the Truth]?"
Master: "Your everyday mind. When I am hungry, I eat; when tired, I sleep."

Here again is the stress on the ordinary and actual which Wittgenstein calls a "form of life" as well as the rejection of the notion of inner states such as mind.

A Zen saying is, "When we are hungry we eat, when sleepy, we lay down—where does the infinite or finite [dualism] come in here?" Intellect supposedly murders. Life as it is lived suffices. "When fish are carried home, don't bother eternally with the basket." Act and do without asking why and so involving ourselves in thinking we are performing a meaningful task when we are not—when as Wittgenstein says,

"The confusions which occupy us arise when language is like an engine idling, not when it is doing work." (PI, 51)

We cannot escape from ordinary language nor can we escape from what we see and do. The Zen man says

"We have to dress and eat every day, and how can we escape from all that?"
Answer: "We dress, we eat."

Wittgenstein similarly says, "What *we* do is to bring words back from their metaphysical to their everyday use." (PI, 116) Just as with ordinary language games what Zen is is itself and nothing more about it can be said.

Monk: "What is Zen?"
Master: "That's it."

That is it and to find out what it is we need only look and see.

"One cannot guess how a word functions. One has to look at its use and learn from that." (PI, 340)

It is what we see around us everyday—what we ordinarily say. It is as we see it in a Haiku—

> "A stray cat
> Asleep on the roof
> In the spring rain."

It is the given. Wittgenstein stresses the given in the following:

"Philosophy may in no way interfere with the actual use of language; it can in the end only describe it. For it cannot give it any foundation either. It leaves everything as it is." (PI, 124)
"Philosophy simply puts everything before us, and neither explains nor deduces anything. Since everything lies open to view, there is nothing to explain." (PI, 126)
"The primitive language-game which children are taught needs no justification; attempts at justification need to be rejected." (PI, 200)
"What has to be accepted, the given, is—so one could say—*forms of life*." (PI, 226)
"But how is this sentence applied—that is, in our everyday language? For I got it from there and nowhere else." (PI, 134)
"When I obey a rule, I do not choose. I obey the rule *blindly*." (PI, 219)
"Our mistake is to look for an explanation where we ought to look at what happens as a 'proto-phenomenon' (a given)." (PI, 654)

The stress on the given is what is indicated in the following Koans

Monk: "Please instruct me in Zen."
Master: "Have you had your breakfast yet or not?"
Monk: "Yes, master, I have."
Master: "If so, have your dishes washed."

"It [life] is like a sword that wounds, but cannot wound itself;
Like an eye that sees, but cannot see itself."

"Nothing whatever is hidden;
From of old, all is clear as daylight."

"The blue hills are of themselves blue hills;
The white clouds are of themselves white clouds."

Monk: "What is Zen?"
Master: "Not a word to be predicated."

Thus both philosophies present us with the view that reality or the actual is a given and nothing can be said about it. Reason and knowing are not relevant to that given. It just is. For Zen even to say anything about Zen is to go wrong. Thus paradox often characterizes the Koan and Zen Haiku. This paradox is not distant from Heraclitus'

"The path up and down is one and the same" and "Mortals are immortals and immortals are mortals, the one living the other's death and dying the other's life."

Paradox often gives us insight, which the Zen sayings meant to do. Contradiction is often at the heart of these Koans. Whatever is said about anything supposedly implies that the opposite may be said also. That Buddha is one implies that he is many. Here again is another instance of breaking down of categories. In this case, the category of contradiction is used to indicate the dissolution, ". . . unravelling complications. . . smoothing out the dust (of discrimination)—this is the mysterious levelling." (cf. Berkeley said that we first raise the dust and then claim that we cannot see.)

"When you have a staff, I will give you one,
When you have none, I will take it away from you."

Consider the following Zen saying:

"One who seeks the Dharma (truth) finds it in seeking it in nothing."

"Only when seeing is no-seeing is there real Zen."

"The cock announces the dawn in the evening.
The sun is bright at midnight."

"The frog
Rises up by the same force
    with which it jumps in." (A Haiku)

"From now on my eyes were one with my ears,
my ears with my nose, my nose with my mouth."

"A long thing is the long body of Buddha.
A short thing is the short body of Buddha."

"There is nothing you see that is not a flower;
there is nothing you can think of which is not the moon."

"A mountain is not high, nor is a pillar vertical."

"Since there is no gate let me tell you how to pass thru it."

"Don't follow sound and chase color. Does the sound come to the side of the ear or the ear to the border of the sound? If one expects to hear the truth with one's ear, it may be difficult to comprehend it. By listening with one's eye, one will for the first time be intimate with it."

"What is Tao?
Ordinary mind is Tao.
Should we try to face it?
Should one try to face it, one deviates from it."

"A robber threatens—there is no robber."

"To be able to trample on the Great Void,
the iron crow must sweat."

"Seeing, they see not;
Hearing, they hear not."

"Where the interplay of 'is' and 'is not' is fixed,
Not even the sages can know."

"Simply you must empty 'is' of meaning,
And not take 'is not' as real."

"It (truth) cannot be attained by mind;
It is not to be sought after through mindlessness."

"It (truth) cannot be created by speech;
It cannot be penetrated by silence."

What characterizes these sayings is an attack on the principle of contradiction, reason, and traditional categories of discrimination. But Wittgenstein attacks at least this much. His view is such that nearly everything that is now thought to be named is no longer a thing. It has meaning and function only as part of a learned, and thus given, language-game—that is, in ordinary language and usage. Memory is no longer a state or process but becomes a word with a use and gains its meaning from that use. Thus "imagination," "understanding," "thought," "mind," no longer stand for internal states. Inner states and processes are categories which as such are dissolved. This, if true, gives support to the Zen attack on certain common definitions and distinctions.

For Wittgenstein, if meaning is use, then the opposing of concepts and the principle of contradiction also becomes undermined. In their place is put models, paradigm cases, and language-games. There are no absolutes which may be once and for all opposed.

"The only correlate in language to an intrinsic necessity is a rule." (PI, 372)

Of the opposition of internal-external, Wittgenstein says, "An inner process stands in need of outward criteria." (PI, 580) What Wittgenstein is saying is that about the internal none of us knows what to say.

If the meaning, for example, of reason and emotion are their uses, then they are not opposed as entities but only as actual uses. But it is not clear that uses can oppose. The same term may be used in many different ways, forms a "family" of uses. It will not do any longer to say that reason as such is opposed to emotion as such. They aren't entities and they aren't single things.

Wittgenstein holds that if you don't have a test, don't say, for example, "Either he thinks or he doesn't." Contradiction doesn't apply here. One may instead say, as the Zen man might, "One thinks and one doesn't think," and that is to say our distinctions break down. Wittgenstein regarded the emulation of private states and the law of non-contradiction as a picture or model which erroneously holds us captive. He wrote,

"For one can quite well call the Law of Contradiction false, on the grounds that we very often make good sense by answering a question 'Yes and no.' " (RFM, 53) and

"If in the midst of life we are in death, so in sanity we are surrounded by madness."
(RFM, 157)

Certainly the history of ideas reveals the constantly changing and under-mining of ideas and principles previously held to be certain, such as the opposition of subject-object, beautiful-ugly, inner-outer, space-time, body-mind, true-false, perceiving-perceived, etc.

The Zen man runs the beautiful and ugly together, and appreciates both.

> "The cow comes
> Moo! Moo!
>   Out of the mist." (A Haiku)
> "The young girl
> Blew her nose
>   In the evening-glory." (A Haiku)

In showing how Wittgenstein rejects certain definitions and distinctions, we may note that his arguments are often as brief and concise as a Koan. The notion of self-identity is regarded as a useless statement.

> "It is as if in imagination we put a thing into its own shape and saw that it fitted."
> (PI, 216)

Also to say that two different things are identical is wrong. ("Roughly speaking, to say of *two* things that they are identical is nonsense, and to say of *one* thing that it is identical with itself is to say nothing at all." *Tractatus*, 5.5303) " 'War is war' is not an example of the law of identity, either." (PI, 221)

All those words which supposedly stand for internal states are analyzed so that they no longer stand for such states. It was mentioned that internal processes stand in need of outward criteria. So also whatever use to which the "mental" can be put, physical things will serve equally well. We speak of inner life with terms used for spatial outer things. Under attack is the notion that there go on in us such processes as knowing, understanding, believing, thinking, remembering, feeling, sensing, intending, meaning, expecting, concentrating, willing, inner or silent speech, hoping, dreaming, judging, and deciding.

Wittgenstein gives some insight into these processes by giving us short tests for and comments about them. His statements are very much like Haikus and Koans in being abrupt and challenging. Consider the following sorts of statements he makes.

Repeating a word again and again shows that in itself, without a use in a situation, it becomes meaningless.

Understanding is an arrow. Consult the arrow, the actual use in language not the "inner thought."

"I see!," "I understand!" are not descriptions of something internal.

Point to two bolts. The pointing seems specific, but how can you define the number two that way rather than just a group.

Point to a piece of paper, then its shape, color, and number. How did you do it? How did you "mean" it? How did you "concentrate" on it?

Don't speak absolutely about the "simple" parts of a chair. Simple depends on a point of view or context.

Don't even look for the essence of a language-game. There is no definite boundary to it.

One sentence is not more fundamental than another.

If to define is to picture, then what shape is green?

I *use* words correctly which I do not know the meaning of.

Augustine: If you ask me (e.g. what time is) I don't know. If you don't ask me, I know.

We also play the game of making up rules as we go along. There is no limit to the uses of language.

"Chair" is also played in the game of thinking of it as an illusion.

"Good" is meaningless until you look and see how you use it.

An explanation averts one misunderstanding that would but for it have occurred—but does not avert every misunderstanding. There are other contexts in which to use "explain."

Stick to the subjects of everyday thinking, otherwise we feel as if we had to repair a torn spider's web with our fingers.

"What is a word really?" is like
"What is a piece in chess?"

Meaning as a picture does not fit meaning as a use.

The picture exists in his imagination? Why not rather a drawing, construction or model in front of him.

When do you know a certain thing?
Day and night? Always? Is knowing a state, one having duration?

When did you stop understanding that word?

Causation doesn't underlie but rather is established by experiments.

Not any one feature occurs in all cases of reading.

I do not feel the movement of the lever which connects seeing the letters with speaking.

Don't think marks make you want to utter certain sounds.

Do you feel the influence of being influenced as you read?

Perhaps the will is not a phenomenon.

I make a movement with my hand. But what is the guiding character of the movement?

A person can look at pointing in reverse, that is, from finger tip to wrist.

The whole act isn't in one when one says, "I know how to go on."

Is the *possibility* of movement
like a shadow of the movement itself?

To know is to act and react, not to give reasons.

The balance on which impressions are weighed is not the impression of a balance.

What are the criteria for remembering a color right?
A memory image cannot be tested for correctness.

It is unverifiable that one section of mankind had one sensation of red and another
section another.

Don't think you read off the rules from the facts.
These rules too would need rules.

To say "I believe he is in pain" is just making a decision to say this instead of "He is
in pain."

How do I know that this color is red?—It would be an answer to say: "I have learnt
English."

We have to deny the yet uncomprehended process in the yet unexplored medium
(mental and other "internal" states).

To be clear about the word "think" don't watch yourself while you think to observe
what the word means.

Was what I was just doing thinking; am I not making a mistake?"

Say: "Yes, this pen is blunt. Oh well, it'll do." First, thinking it; then without
thought; then just think the thought without the words. Can you?

Do words occur in the order one thinks them?

Did I really intend the whole construction of the sentence at its beginning?

A machine can't think because it has no place to think. But neither does man.

Can you point to imagination?

What is the meaning of "*this* image?" Can you point to one? The same one twice?

Do you "possess" thought?

The "visual room" seemed like a discovery but it is just a new way of speaking.

"I am. . . . " "I" doesn't name anyone here. (cf. Selflessness)

What does certainty really amount to: If I put my hand in the fire I get burned.

What does a man think for? What use is it?

Does it follow from the sense-impressions which I get that there is a chair over there?
How can a proposition follow from sense impressions?

Say "It's cold here" and mean
"It's warm here." Can you?

Is negation a mental activity?

Mental is not a presupposition we must make.

Does some feature of our memory image tell us the time to which it belongs?

I can only see, not hear, red and green—but sadness I can hear as much as I can see it. Sadness is walking down a long grey tunnel.

He senses the truth. With which sense?

Above all, don't wonder "What can be going on in the eyes and brain?" in order to analyze the meaning of a word.

Is your thought as long as your sentence?

You can calculate in your head?
Can you decorate the wall in your head?

Does "He can play chess" name a state?

Can you remember what remembering was like last Tuesday?

It would not be correct to say, as we did earlier, that Wittgenstein rejects all inner states or that he is consistent in rejecting them or that he is consistent in everything he says. He is not, depending upon which way we look at what he wrote. However, establishing consistency is not the task here. We may look at each statement Wittgenstein makes as a separate model or paradigm case. Wittgenstein in his preface to the *Investigations* says that his remarks are a number of sketches of landscapes made in the course of long and involved journeyings.

In any case, the above statements show how Wittgenstein set about to undo a great number of pictures of reality which we are, he thinks, captivated by. It has that in common with Zen. Instead of resting secure with a partial view of, for example, "mental entities," the notion is placed in a total and living context or form of life. Notions are brought back to the whole context also in Zen.

The character and nature of the Koan and Haiku are similar to Wittgenstein's writings also in that contexts and concepts are combined which are not usually associated with one another. This either exposes commonly accepted and literally accepted notions to meaninglessness or gives us insight into their meaning. A large number of statements we utter are seen to be disguised forms of jokes. Wittgenstein once said that a serious and good philosophical work could be written that would consist entirely of jokes.[9] And, "My aim is: to teach you to pass from a piece of disguised nonsense to something that is patent nonsense." (PI, 464) The humor involved is, as mentioned earlier, a kind of therapy which reveals where we go wrong. The mistakes involve misleading grammatical parallels, category mistakes of various sorts or, in general, conceptual confusion. Wittgenstein talks of "Misunderstandings concerning the use of words, caused, among other things, by certain analogies between the forms of expression in different regions of language." (PI, 90) We know that such statements as the following are not correct but there are other incorrectly used expressions which escape our notice.

---

[9] Norman Malcolm, *Ludwig Wittgenstein: A Memoir*, p. 29.

What is the sum of two plus apples?
She sat down grammatically.
He has five cents in his pocket grammatically.
I rode my bicycle in French.
The number seven hurts.
I have N friends and $N^2 + 2N + 2 = 0$

Such context confusion involves for instance talking of inner life in terms used for spatial outer things. But Wittgenstein's insights and humor center around breaking loose from traditional categories by comparing concepts not previously compared. Malcolm related how Wittgenstein to effectively wash dinner dishes in appreciation of Malcolm's hospitality thought nothing of sweeping the dishes off to the bathtub to do an effective washing job.

We saw some of the ways in which this washing job was done on the mind. Zen does a similar job using a similar method and arrives at a notion of man not too different in a way—a doctrine of no-mind, selflessness. Examples of Wittgenstein's humor follow. Most examples are his own. The first ones indicate statements which seem parallel but aren't but the grammar misleads us into thinking they are. When we see that they are misleading, we see that they involve a disguised joke. In all these cases, the first sentence or word is not like the second.

My mind is made up (is not like)
My bed is made up.
I multiplied in my head.
I multiplied in room #23.
I calculated in my head.
I calculated on paper.
Inner speech.
Whispering.
A thought flashed through his head.
A star flashed through the sky.
I observe my consciousness.
I observe my actions.
Memory.
Looking down a spy glass.
The meaning of a word.
The illustration of a story.
I mean something.
I say something.
Where is your mind?
Where is your book?
Where is your pain?
Where is your pen?
The present event passes by.
A log passes by.
A minute passes by.
A car passes by.
Who made the world?
Who made the shoes?
Where is your intelligence?
Where is your book?

Your mind is in your head.
Your apples are in your pail.
    A man is (at all).
    A man is there.
What are you for?
What is your eraser for?
    Where did the time go?
    Where did the paper go?
He said in his mind '340.'
He said in Russian '340.'
    Thinking is a process.
    Digestion is a process.
He digests his ideas.
He digests food.
    What's on your mind?
    What's on the stove?
Things are stored in your memory.
Things are stored in a warehouse.
    I saw him in a dream.
    I saw him in the theatre.
I consulted my imagination.
I consulted a timetable.

The following Zen sayings reflect several types of humor, for instance, incongruity, repeating the question, answering what is irrelevant. It might be appropriate on Wittgenstein's view to take "Shut up" or "I don't know" as appropriate answers to questions which are meaningless or misleading such as "Where is your mind?"[10] (Since an answer such as "My mind is in my head and I think with it" is unenlightening, one may as well answer, as the Zen man does, something quite irrelevant.) Several typical humorous Zen sayings follow.

Monk: "What I wish to know is where is Nansen gone after his death?"
Master: "As to that it makes one think."

Monk: "What I wish to know is where is Nansen gone after his death?"
Master: "When Sekito was still in the order of young novitiates, he saw the sixth patriarch."

Monk: "What is the fundamental teaching of the Buddha?"
Master: "Is there enough breeze in this fan to keep me cool?"

Monk: "What is Zen?"
Master: "It is cloudy today and I won't answer."

Monk: "What is Buddhahood?"
Master: "The bottom of a pail is broken through?"

Monk: "What is Zen?"
Master: "Zen."

Monk: "Please instruct me in Zen."
Master: "Have you had your breakfast yet or not?"
Monk: "Yes, master, I have."
Master: "If so, have your dishes washed."

---

[10]Wittgenstein is reported to have actually said such a thing in his lectures on Philosophical Psychology.

"In the garden
the camellia is blooming
    whitely." (A Haiku)

"They spoke no word,
The visitor, the host,
    And the white chrysanthemum." (A Haiku)

"The sea darkens:
Voices of the wild ducks
    Are faintly white." (A Haiku)

The three preceding Haiku's indicate a breaking out into striking usages which, although they are misuses, may serve as useful models or hypotheses. Why doesn't a camellia bloom whitely? Is blue a noun by nature? In some languages we say "It blues." Are we misled by grammar, thinking that blue is substantive rather than a process or action?

There is, of course, some humor in the Zen statements quoted earlier which serves to undermine distinctions and oppositions. For example:

"A long thing is the long body of Buddha.
A short thing is the short body of Buddha."

The quotations of both philosophies have a number of different meanings and uses not all of which can be explored here. Both philosophies stress giving free play to the creative impulses. Wittgenstein's models or paradigm cases and examples of misleading parallels are revealing as are statements of a Koan and Haiku.

One sort of notion both philosophies give insight into is that of "explanation" or "cause." A Zen analysis runs,

1. The pennant is inanimate and it is the wind that makes it flap.
2. Both wind and pennant are inanimate and flapping is impossibility.
3. The flapping is due to a certain combination of cause and condition.
4. After all there is no flapping pennant, but it is the wind that is moving by itself.
5. It is neither wind nor pennant but your mind that flaps.

Since the stress is on actual speech and action, "cause" and "explanation" are more *part* of such actions than simple reports of it. Wittgenstein attacks internal states as causes of behavior as well as the notion of cause as divorced from our ordinary use of the word: the case is the same with the meaning of words like "explain."

To say X causes Y is not necessarily to give a report or make a claim about the existence of causality. It is rather to know when we use the word, cause. One view Wittgenstein has is, then, that there is no real cause, explanation, or influence. There is no explanation for explanation. We cannot explain the meanings of words. We can merely use them. Another way to say this is that "cause" *shows* itself by its use but it has no essential definition. This is in line with the view held by both philosophies that it is showing (doing), not telling (explaining) which is important. Such words as cause and explain, like "language" and "experience," are often thought of as being of a higher level than words like "book" and "chair." Wittgenstein, however, says, "If the words 'language,' 'experience,' 'world,' have a use, it must be as humble a one as that of the words 'table,' 'lamp,' 'door.' " (PI, 97) We are reminded again of the statement that "Philosophy may in no way interfere with the actual use of language; it can in the end only describe it. For it cannot give it any foundation either. It leaves everything as it is." (PI, 124) And ". . . 'Have I reasons?' The answer is: my reasons will soon give out. And then I shall act, without reasons." (PI, 211)

It is not the case that causality has one meaning (use) but rather that there are as many meanings as uses—as many models of cause as we wish to find. The Zen approach is similar in its stress on the many aspects of each thing we consider. In neither philosophy are we allowed to be held captive by a single picture, or distinction. It is, as we mentioned, a philosophic disease to be able to see only one kind of model. The model Wittgenstein thought us most mistakenly addicted to is that of naming—that words supposedly name entities. (In Zen, naming is opposed also, because it leads to dualism.) For both philosophies there is not just one way or aspect. (cf, PI, 91) There is no final way, no final demonstration.

PB-39393-SB
741-44T
5